BOOK THREE

Religion for a Change

An Integrated Course in Religious and Personal Education

Martin Palmer
Joanne O'Brien
Elizabeth Breuilly

ICOREC
International Consultancy on Religion, Education and Culture

Stanley Thornes (Publishers) Ltd

First published in 1991 by:
Stanley Thornes (Publishers) Ltd
Old Station Drive
Leckhampton
CHELTENHAM GL53 0DN
England

British Library Cataloguing in Publication Data

Palmer, Martin
Religion for a change: book 3: An integrated course in religious and personal education.
I. Title II. O'Brien, Joanne
III. Breuilly, Elizabeth
291.07

ISBN 0-7487-0475-2

Designed by Claire Brodmann
Typeset by Tech-Set, Gateshead, Tyne & Wear
Printed and bound in Hong Kong

Acknowledgements

The authors and the publishers are grateful to the following for permission to reproduce photographs:

Alcoholics Anonymous page 39
Associated Press page 83
Stephen Batchelor page 85
Bristol United Press page 64
CAFOD page 6
Dean and Chapter Canterbury Cathedral page 33
Dean and Chapter Durham Cathedral page 30
Foundation de Bellerive page 5
Health Education Authority page 40
ICOREC pages 16, 27, 47
LIV Communications SA pages 7, 8, 9
Mary Evans Picture Library page 35
Midland Bank plc page 62
National Anti-vivisection Society page 86
National Westminster Bank plc page 62
Pictor International page 56
The Salvation Army page 75
United Nations Information Centre page 91
Visual Arts Library pages 20, 67, 69, 87
WWF UK page 30
York and County Press page 88

The publishers have made every effort to contact copyright holders and apologise if any have been overlooked.

Illustrations by Carol Ann Duncombe and Fran Orford

Many people and groups have helped us with comments and ideas in the preparation of this book. In particular we thank the following teachers who spent many hours discussing the concept with us as it took shape:
Janet Buck
Liz Collins
Angus McCormick
David White

Contents

INTRODUCTION

The Role-play Sections

In each chapter of this book you will find sources from different religions and each set of sources is related to the topic of that chapter. These sources give you a glimpse of what each faith teaches about a particular subject, but what does this mean in practice? The role-plays are included to help you find this out.

The sources give background information for the role-plays. We provide specific situations to which you have to respond. In some of the role-plays you have to imagine you are a member of a particular faith and decide what a believer of that faith would do. If you are doing this as a group, try to cover as many different faiths as possible within the group. Remember, it is important to put yourself into somebody else's shoes and to argue from their standpoint. For example, if you are pretending to be a Buddhist monk you will have to try to think like one. This will mean imagining that you are poor and humble, which is not always easy! Or if you are St Francis of Assisi at the time of the Crusades, act peacefully and without violence. Do not act out of character or time, such as St Francis being confronted by a horde of enemy soldiers and suddenly finding a sub-machine gun up his habit!

The role-plays can be used as drama or written work. If you are doing this as a drama role-play, try to be sensitive to the kind of person you are playing. If you are doing this through written work, treat the views of the faiths with respect.

Sometimes you are asked to take on the role of someone in a particular job, or a particular situation, rather than a religion. In the same way, you must try to be true to what that person would think and do, rather than what you think yourself. For example, the managing director of a firm selling chocolate is not likely to give chocolate to anyone who cannot pay for it!

You will need to work on preparing for your role: find out what your character thinks and believes, plan what you are going to say, and think what arguments might be used against you and what

your answers would be. Sometimes you will find this easy, because you agree with the view you are expressing. It is more difficult to play a role with which you disagree but you may learn more from it.

At the end of the role-play, the teacher will ask you to discuss what went on. How did you feel? Were you satisfied with how you presented your case? Did anyone win the argument? Were you convinced by the arguments of another person?

So when you are role-playing, it is as though you were two people. There is the character you have 'become' for the time being. This character is very important: treat him or her with great respect. But in the background there is always the 'real' you – watching, criticising and learning.

ENVIRONMENT

The Challenge

'You've done some stupid things in your life Karen, but this really is the most stupid,' said Karen's mother. 'And why the others' parents are letting them do this, I do not know. Don't come crying to me if you catch cold or some other illness.'

It had been going on like this ever since Karen had come home and announced what she was going to do. The others had a similar problem. And it had all started as a joke.

It had been a wet dinner time at school. The class had sat around feeling gloomy. For lack of anything better to do, Karen had said 'I feel about as happy as I would sitting in a cold bath.' Well, trust Caroline to rise to this.

'And how would you know what that felt like? When did you last sit in a cold bath?'

There is no need to go into all the discussion that followed. But at the end, for reasons that she could never properly explain, Karen had agreed to a challenge. The challenge was that Caroline would give £20 to any charity Karen named, if Karen would sit in a cold bath for at least an hour. Rather a stupid idea you might think. So did Karen when she realised what she had agreed to in the heat of the argument.

That Sunday at church, the vicar was talking about the environment. It seemed that Christian Aid was trying to raise money to fund tree nurseries in different parts of the world and to buy fuel-economic stoves in order to cut down on the amount of firewood people had to burn to cook their food. In the youth group after church, Karen suggested that they should try to raise funds through a sponsored event.

'Oh, Karen, that's been done to death,' said Mike. 'Sponsored runs, sponsored walks – everyone's tired of them. There's nothing new.' It was then that Karen had a brain wave.

'How about a sponsored cold bath?' she said.

'Oh, Karen, do grow up!' said Julie. 'You'll be suggesting sitting in cold custard next!'

'No, I'm serious!' said Karen. 'I had a challenge with a friend at school, but this is different. Look, what we're trying to do here is encourage people in other countries not to waste fuel, because it destroys the forests. But how can we say that when we ourselves are wasting so much? It's only a small thing, I know, but if some of us promise to wash only in cold water for a month, at least we're doing something, and we could raise money by sponsorship – so much per day without hot water.'

Several of the group shuddered at that – but they had to admit it was a challenge.

At home, they met with a mixed reaction.

'If you really want to shiver, then shiver,' said Karen's mum. 'But don't think you'll get away with not washing at all, my girl. I'll expect to see you pink and scrubbed and shining every morning.'

'Don't you mean blue?' chipped in her brother.

Julie's parents would not hear of it.

'It's all very well in hot countries, but this is England in October. You'll catch your death,' said her mum.

'But I must do something – something that shows I'm serious about saving fuel. I know! You always complain that you drive two miles out of your way to drop me at school. How about if I walk, or get the bus instead? Would you sponsor that?'

And so the idea grew. Different people came up with different ideas for saving fuel and being sponsored to raise money for environmental projects in the Third World. But of course it was the cold baths that received the most attention. Soon the local radio station heard about it. They invited Karen to the studios for an interview about it. Because she had never done an interview before, she took Padma with her and Joseph asked if he could come too. Well, Karen soon proved not to be very good at interviews. All she could manage was 'Yes' or 'No'. In desperation the interviewer turned to Joseph and Padma.

'So, why are you two joining this?'

Now neither Padma nor Joseph had any intention of joining in! But they could not really say that, could they? Especially as Joseph belonged to the RSPB and Padma had recently joined Friends of the Earth. So, to Karen's considerable astonishment, her two friends rose to the occasion magnificently.

'I shall be doing it to protest against the destruction of the rainforests,' said Padma. 'Did you know that we are in danger of destroying all the rainforests of the world within my lifetime! If we do that, the world will begin to die because the great forests give us oxygen. They help protect us, so we must protect them. As a Buddhist, I follow the Lord Buddha's teaching that we should care for all life.'

Joseph, not to be outdone, chipped in: 'I shall be doing it because of the thousands of species of birds which have already been wiped out and the thousands that are at risk. I want my children and their children to see the beautiful birds I see. I wish I could have seen some of the birds which are now extinct. How can I not act? God gave us this world to look after. I don't think our end of term report to God looks very good at the moment. It may not seem much having a few cold baths – but if it makes some people stop and think, then I'll do it.'

They were into their stride and the poor interviewer did not stand a chance.

'So come on everyone out there,' said Padma. 'Support us this next month. But don't just give money – read all about what is happening to our world. Join Greenpeace or WWF and find out.'

'And think what you could do,' said Joseph. 'Maybe you could help raise funds or give some time to help in our neighbourhood. If you've got any ideas, ring us at the station and let us know what you plan to do.'

The interviewer interrupted quickly. 'Yes folks, give us a ring in the next hour and let's get this going. Thank you all for coming in and I hope we can chat again soon. Now our next track is . . .'

As they left the station Karen said 'Are you really going to join us?' 'Looks like we haven't got much option now,' laughed Padma. 'But the money is going to Christian Aid,' said Karen. 'Don't worry, I don't think the rabbi will disown me. I think he would have disowned me if I didn't join in!' said Joseph.

Information boxes

Tree Nurseries and Fuel-Economic Stoves

Fuel-economic stove in use in Kenya

One of the major causes of environmental destruction is the loss of trees. There are many reasons for this, such as intensive farming and wood being used for cooking. The result is that trees are cut down and the soil is farmed, even though the soil is often too poor. Because of the loss of trees, water is not retained by the soil but runs off it and often washes the soil away as well.

Two major ways of trying to change this have been developed. The first is the planting of new trees. To do this, young saplings have to be raised, which involves the tree nurseries. They develop saplings from seed and will advise on which trees are best for which area. In many parts of the world, religious communities have developed tree nurseries and provide thousands of trees to farmers. The second is the fuel-economic stove. This is a simple idea but a difficult one to get adopted. Over the last decade, experiments have taken place which have produced the most efficient stove possible. The stoves use wood, for in many parts of the world there is no other fuel. The fuel economic stoves can cut the amount of firewood needed by nearly 40 per cent.

Development Agencies and Ecology

Over the last few years, development agencies such as Oxfam, Catholic Fund for Overseas Development (CAFOD) and Christian Aid, have begun to introduce environmental issues into their programmes. They now run major environmental projects and some of them ensure that all new development programmes have assessed the environmental impact of new housing or intensive farming, for example. But problems often still occur. The demands of the human population on a fragile environment cannot be easily resolved. All the major development agencies have literature on their environmental work which can be ordered from their headquarters. It is worth studying to see the problems as well as some of the solutions.

A campaign poster by CAFOD

Activities

1. Padma and Joseph gave reasons on the radio for helping environmental concerns. Write down in your own words what these reasons were.
2. What would Karen, as a Christian, have liked to say about her reasons? Use the Sources on page 10 to help you.
3. What types of fuel can be saved by
   a) not using so much hot water?
   b) walking instead of going by car?
   Where does this fuel come from?
4. Find out how a fuel-economic stove works. Or design one yourself.
5. Write an advertising brochure explaining why fuel-economic stoves are worth using.
6. Make a display of information about different environmental organisations. What does each one do? Why do they do it? Where do they get their money from? How is it spent? Write to organisations such as Oxfam, Christian Aid and CAFOD for material on their environmental programmes.

The Forest and the Monk

Ajahn Pongsak standing in a dried-up river bed

Ever since he could remember Ajahn Pongsak had wanted to be a Buddhist monk. But he was not interested in the easy life of the city monks. He wanted to be a forest monk. This meant spending up to three months a year in the forests of Thailand, meditating quietly in the solitude of the great forests. For hundreds of years, this peaceful life had gone on and Ajahn Pongsak wished to be part of it. To his joy he was accepted and began his lifelong journey of meditation and prayer.

Within a quite short period of time he was widely respected as a teacher. At an early age he became Ajahn – which means Abbot or Leader of a community of monks.

But something else was happening too. Life was becoming difficult for the forest monks because the forests were disappearing. At first, only a few people noticed. The logging companies were growing larger year by year. Foreign companies came in with bigger machines. But Thailand had lots of forest, so what was there to worry about?

By the time most people became aware of the environmental destruction, it was too late to save most of the forest. In 30 years more than 50 per cent of the forests of Thailand had disappeared. With no forests to hold the water, the streams and rivers dried up. Farmers found their fields could not be watered so crops did not grow and food ran short. The wonderful wildlife simply disappeared in much of the country.

The forest monks had noticed the destruction of the forests. They were finding it harder and harder to find places to go to meditate. One year they would be deep in the heart of an ancient forest and by the following year their meditations were disturbed by the noise of the loggers. A year later and their forest was gone all together. The monks were upset, but they felt that it was not their job to do anything. That was not the role of the monk.

Ajahn Pongsak felt differently. He saw the destruction of the forest where he used to go to meditate; he saw the deaths of thousands of animals and he saw the distress of the farmers and their families. As a Buddhist he had compassion for all those who were suffering. And so he decided that as a monk, he had to set an example. What good was it to believe in compassion but not to practise it? What good was it to teach compassion but not to help people actually live compassionately?

In the Mae Soi Valley, not far from the temple where he was the abbot or ajahn, was a valley that had been completely deforested. The three original streams which watered the farmers' fields had shrunk to one. Here, the Ajahn began to teach the Buddhist villagers why the streams had dried up. He explained to them how to begin tree replanting schemes.

The villagers were puzzled. This monk did not act like other monks. He did not seem to be doing any harm, but there were often policemen and government agents checking up on his activities. And they heard tales of how he was plotting to overthrow the government. But gradually, they began to listen to his teachings and with his help, began to put them into practice. They had never met a monk like this, but they rallied round him. And soon they found how difficult things can become when you try to turn the tide of events and when money is involved. As word of Ajahn Pongsak's actions spread – first within Thailand and then abroad – he came under fierce attack.

Attacks began on Ajahn Pongsak in the newspapers which supported the government. They claimed that no ordinary forest monk would behave like him and that he was not, in fact, a monk at all. They claimed he was not a Buddhist but a Communist sent to overthrow the government of Thailand. They hinted that they had ways of dealing with people who stood in their way. The papers labelled him a trouble-maker. The loggers threatened the villagers and the monks, the hill tribes tried black magic – all in the attempt to stop Ajahn Pongsak. But nothing would deter him.

Soon, monks and ordinary people from all over Thailand came to visit his ecological monastery. Similar places were also set up. Even the king of Thailand heard of his work. And slowly, very slowly, things began to change. Ajahn Pongsak knows that he may have been too late – but as a Buddhist and as a monk, he knows he must continue to show, in his life and work, the power of the Buddha's compassion for all life on earth.

Activities

1. What do you think Ajahn Pongsak might have said to the villagers to explain his activities and his Buddhist beliefs? Write a conversation between Ajahn Pongsak and some of the villagers.
2. Why do you think the government did not like his activities?
3. Are there any natural areas of land that you remember seeing when you were younger which have now disappeared? What has taken their place?

Ajahn Pongsak and local villagers

Before deforestation

4. Have green areas been created in your local area? What can you find there?
5. Find out the names of local environmental groups. What work do they do? Try to organise a class project to help one of these groups.

After deforestation

Sources

BUDDHISM

The Buddhist attitude to nature is one of great compassion. Buddhism teaches that we are all linked by the cycle of rebirth. Buddhism teaches that everything in the world is trapped in a life of suffering. So to see any real difference between, for example, an animal and a human being, is foolish. All life needs love, compassion and help to overcome suffering. Buddhism also teaches karma. This means that whatever we do to something, we will eventually feel the effect of our actions. This is why if we harm a creature, we will eventually suffer as a result of that. If we cut down trees, then we will suffer too. The soil will wash away, there will be less oxygen in the air and life will become even more difficult. So for karma reasons we should never take lives of anything if we can avoid it. But above and beyond this, the Buddha has shown that everyone should show compassion.

Buddhism teaches a practical path to caring for the world by suggesting living the life of holy simplicity. To take and use only what you really need would solve the economic and environmental problems of many countries almost overnight!

CHRISTIANITY

Christians believe that people have been given special power and authority over the world and all life on it. This power and authority means we have to look after all life on earth and use it with care. The world does not belong to us, but is entrusted to us.

Nature, creation, is here not only to be useful to people. It is here because God loves all of creation and cares for every part of it. As Jesus said, 'Can you not buy two sparrows for a penny? And yet not one falls to the ground without your Father knowing.'

Christians believe that the world is here for us to use, but in using it we must take care of it. Everything we need to live is provided for us. Our role is to use it and replenish or replace what we use. Some Christians talk about us being co-creators with God. We are here to make creation even better. Cities, music, art, language, drama – all these human inventions are part of our being creators with God of an even more beautiful and marvellous world. But human beings can also bring destruction, greed, war and death to the world. For this reason, Christians believe Jesus Christ came to show us how to live and to bring peace and reconciliation to all creation.

So for Christians, creation is loved by God, provided for our use, but to be cared for because God cares for it. But most of all, creation does not belong to us. As the psalm says: 'The Earth is the Lord's and everything in the world' (Psalm 24).

HINDUISM

At the heart of Hinduism lies a simple yet profound teaching. It is that in all aspects of life, from the most humble plant through the vast array of animals and birds to the human race, there is the same kind of 'soul' known as the atman. This atman suffers and experiences life in exactly the same way. The fact that some atmans are clothed in the body of an ant, water lily, monkey, elephant or human being is irrelevant. All atmans are on a journey through life after life until eventually they can return to their original source – the Supreme One. As the Bhagavad Gita says: 'The wise look upon a Brahman full of learning and humility, a cow, an elephant, a dog and the lowest kind of human being, as being the same.'

Like Buddhists, Hindus believe that what you do now will shape what happens to you in the future – karma. As vegetarians, they point to one example of how foolish, greedy behaviour has returned to affect us all. They look at some people's love of meat, such as hamburgers. This meat eating is very distressing to Hindus for the reasons given above. They point out that to cater for people's desire for meat, vast areas of the Amazonian forest have been destroyed to provide ranches for the cattle to graze on. Once the cattle have grazed, they destroy any chance of the forest growing again. This destruction of the rain forests is now causing global warming and flooding. Many Hindus believe that the bad karmic behaviour of meat eating is now coming back to haunt us.

ISLAM

The core of Islamic teaching rests on belief in Allah as the Creator. He made everything and keeps everything in its place. Humanity is the most special creation of Allah, because we are the only creatures to whom Allah has given the power of reason and the means to think. We are the only species which can look at something and decide to do one of two things – that which is right or that which is wrong. Muslims say this means we have the power to rise higher than the angels or sink lower than the lowest beast.

Islam teaches that God has made us 'khalifas'. This means we are like vice-regents. When a mighty emperor has many lands, he appoints vice-regents to govern the different lands. They do not own the land as it all belongs to the emperor. The job of the vice-regent is to rule the land in the name of the emperor and to treat all those who live in the land as the emperor would treat them. We know that Allah wishes us to care for all creatures even though he has also told us to make use of them. So if we misuse or abuse animals, or the birds of the air, or even the waters of the seas, we are not caring for them as Allah wishes us to. This means we have disobeyed Allah and we will be punished in the future.

Islam continued

The Qur'an also teaches that Allah is interested and cares for all creatures. The Qur'an says that animals live in communities just like humans do. Anyone who damages such a community will be judged by Allah in the afterlife.

Muhammad said, 'Created beings are the dependants of Allah, so the creature dearest to Allah is he who does most good to Allah's dependants'. As 'khalifas' of Allah, we must look after this world in such a way as to show that Allah is Lord of all and we are only his servants. Islam means submission. We need to submit to Allah's will for all his creation and treat it with the respect and care Allah expects.

Role-play

1. A proposal has been made to ban all hunting. Parliament has decided that it should be put to the vote by the people. A nationwide campaign has begun to try to argue the case. The hunting lobby point out that had it not been for hunters, most of the English countryside would have been deforested and farmed leaving no place for wildlife. They also point out that they do not hunt endangered species and that many of the birds they hunt would not exist in such numbers if they were not deliberately bred for hunting. They also point out that hunting can often mean a quicker death than the death of a cow or sheep in the slaughterhouse. They also say that the animals they hunt lead a normal, wild existence before their death, unlike battery hens, for example.

Imagine you are a journalist on a religious newspaper. Choose which faith you represent, making sure that several different faiths are represented in the class. You have been asked to write this week's editorial on the theme of the hunting ban. You know that the debate is getting quite heated. What would you write and how would you present your case to your fellow believers?

2. You are a member of a local community which has many people living in very bad housing. There are not many jobs in your area and the range of shops is very poor. Suddenly a foreign business group decides to build a new factory on meadows and woodlands on the edge of your town. They plan to build new houses, new roads, a big new shopping centre and to create over 600 permanent new jobs. The local conservation action group is against them. They do not want the factory, houses or a shopping centre and believe the new roads will mean more cars and pollution. They want the meadows and woodland preserved to protect a rare flower which grows in the woodland.

A public meeting has been called. All the religious leaders in the area have been contacted by both the company and the conservation action group, asking the leaders to support their case.

First of all, decide what each letter would say to the different religious leaders, using ideas drawn from the beliefs of the particular faith. Then decide which side your character would take in the public meeting and then hold a mock public meeting to see what happens. Make sure there are also people to represent the points of view of the company and the action group. Take a vote at the end to see who wins.

3. Imagine you are head of a galactic empire. You have the greatest scientists in the universe at your command. They have discovered how to create life and build entire new worlds.

You have decided to build a new planet. It will be very similar to a legendary planet once known to have existed on the edge of your galaxy and which was known as the Earth by its inhabitants and as Planet 4 by everyone else! The planet will have land with vegetation and wildlife on it. There will also be oceans. There will be millions of species of animals in the air, on land and in the waters, none of which will look exactly like the ones which once lived on Earth. To run the planet you can create one creature more powerful than any others. However, you know that Earth, or Planet 4, was destroyed by the stupidity and bad behaviour of the most powerful species - humans.

First, design the planet and describe or draw some of the creatures you have invented to live on the planet. Secondly, draw up a set of rules by which your most powerful species must live in order to use, but not destroy, the other species or the planet. In making up these rules, look at the teachings of the different faiths and see what rules they have which you think might work.

The Answer

'Please, Christine, come with me!' pleaded Caroline. 'I can't possibly go on my own, and I've just got to talk to him.'

'I can't, Caro, I really can't. My dad would hit the roof. Look, you don't know what goes on in there. I've heard some funny stories. Couldn't you just forget the whole thing? Why is it so important?'

'There are things I never said, that needed saying. I have to know that he understands, that he's OK where he is now.'

'Caroline,' said Christine gently, 'Your grandad's dead. Nothing will bring him back now. Let him go. I'm sure he understands, whatever it was. But there's no way I'm going to set foot in that Spiritualist meeting. It's spooky. And anyway, it's all a load of nonsense. If your grandad wants to tell you anything, why would he need to send messages through that woman who calls herself a medium? Why doesn't he just come back and haunt you?'

Christine had meant that as a joke, to try to make Caroline smile. But when she saw the expression on Caroline's face, she realised that she had only made matters worse.

'You're right, Christine, you're right!' Caroline whispered. 'He'd talk to me, I know he would! We don't need to go to any meeting, we can have our own. There would have to be a few of us; I don't think these things work on your own. Look, my parents are out next Friday, the house would be quiet. Couldn't you get some of our friends to come round and try it? I can't ask them myself, it means too much to me. I couldn't stand it if they laughed. But you could get some of them together, couldn't you? Please, Christine, please!'

Christine did not really know how seriously to take this. But she thought it could not do any harm, a few of them just sitting round at Caroline's house, and maybe talking a bit about her grandfather. And as for anything else – well, you never know, and it could be interesting to see what happened. So in the end, she invited Colin and Dave, because she thought it would be rather nice to sit round and talk with them, especially with Colin. But she was a bit vague when she told them why they were going.

'Well, you know Caroline's been a bit down since her grandad died, wishes she could still talk to him, and that. So I said we'd go round and help her out, OK?'

They were shocked when they arrived at Caroline's house, and realised how seriously she was taking this. The curtains were drawn in the sitting room, and the light was turned down very low. Four chairs were arranged round the table.

'Hey, wait a minute!', said Dave, 'what's going on here?'

'Shut up, Dave!' said Christine under her breath. 'Just go along with it, can't you?'

Colin, too, was beginning to look a little bit worried, but when Caroline said they should all sit round, and put their hands on the table, with the fingers touching, he made sure he sat next to Christine, and seemed happy enough.

'Now concentrate,' said Caroline, and they sat there in silence. Christine reckoned that as Caroline had not said what they were to concentrate on, she was free to think her own thoughts – so she spent quite a bit of time concentrating on Colin sitting beside her, and wondering what he thought. But as time went by, the atmosphere in the room began to feel uncomfortable. Dave had never really wanted to join in with this, and he began to feel nervous. And like many people, when he got nervous, he got silly. He let out a little giggle.

'Is there anybody there?' he intoned in a dramatic voice. 'Tell me, oh spirits of the dead, tell me . . .' he paused a minute, trying to think of something silly to ask, so they could all laugh and forget the whole thing. 'Tell me,' he found himself saying, 'when will I die?'

Caroline snatched her hands back from the table and burst into tears. And for a moment the other two were too busy comforting her to notice Dave's reaction. For he had also snatched his hands back and was sitting bolt upright, white and shaking. Then he rushed out of the room, and would have rushed out of the house, but just at that moment, Caroline's parents returned. Dave was too scared to know who he was talking to.

'I heard him!' he gasped, 'didn't you? Didn't you hear a voice say 'Soon!' Christine, didn't you hear it?'

'I – I don't know,' faltered Christine. 'I heard something – I think.'

When Caroline's dad had calmed them down and they told him what had been going on, he was very angry.

'How dare you play on my daughter's feelings like that! You know she's upset! Get out of my house, all of you.'

They were all too shaken to explain that they had not meant any harm, and they slunk from the house in silence, hoping they could just forget the whole thing. But Dave could not forget what he had heard. By Monday night, he was very anxious and nervous. Colin took him to Christine's house, and they sat in her bedroom and tried to reason with him.

'Look,' said Christine, 'we don't believe in spirits or ghosts, do we? So what are you getting so worked up about?'

'It was hot in there,' said Colin. 'We were all keyed up. Maybe you didn't really hear anything at all.'

But Dave became more and more upset, so Christine brought her mum upstairs to see him. When she found out what had been going on she was cross.

'You stupid fools! Don't play around with things you don't understand!'

'But Mum,' protested Christine, 'you don't believe in religious, superstitious things!'

'Christine,' said her mum sharply, 'there are very deep and strange forces that run through what people call the spirit world. I don't believe most of the stories, but I do believe powers can be released in some way if you play with such things. Dave needs help on this. I know – I'll ring my friend, Steve Benton. He's dealt with all sorts of problems at that advice centre he works for. We'll see if he can help.' Steve was an old family friend. Christine had always felt that she could talk to him and that his advice was worth listening to.

That night, two very long discussions took place. A very frightened Dave and Christine talked late into the night with her mum and Steve Benton. Meanwhile, over at Caroline's house, her dad sat and talked with Caroline. For by now, Caroline was not sure what she believed – only that some things are best left unknown, and that there was no easy answer to her feelings about her grand-father.

Information box

Spiritualism

Spiritualists believe that the essential part of a person, that which makes them more than just a physical body, lives on after death in a world which is somehow linked with this physical world. Because of this connection people can become aware of those who have died, through various psychic means such as telepathy, clairvoyance, or even by the dead appearing to people. Spiritualists believe that everyone has some ability to be aware of the presence of those who have died. In some people this ability is more marked, and can be cultivated and trained. These people are called mediums. Mediums may offer to help other people by showing evidence that people do survive after death, or by putting them in contact with loved ones who have died.

Members of some faiths, particularly many Christians, believe that although people do live on after their death, it is wrong to try to contact them, since this is breaking the barrier that God has put between this world and the next.

It is generally accepted by spiritualists and non-spiritualists that these are areas which are not fully understood and where it can be very dangerous to play games or experiment without proper guidance.

Activities

1. Why do you think Caroline was so anxious to contact her grandfather?
2. Using the story, information box and your own imagination, script or act out the two conversations described in the last paragraph of the story.
3. Now write the ending to the story that *you* believe is most likely. Does anything happen to Dave or does his life go on as normal?
4. After you have decided your ending, explain why you believe that it is the most likely ending.

Star Letters

The *Weekly Bugle* is a rather old-fashioned newspaper. It only comes out once a week and serves a small market town and the surrounding area. Its greatest claim to fame is that in 1834 it exposed a bank fraud in the area and this led to the arrest of the directors of the bank. Since then, things had been rather quiet.

Then Jeremy Armstrong moved into the area. He was a well-known TV personality and he specialised in horoscopes and had once had his own slot on a breakfast TV programme. Now he appeared as a guest on chat shows and wrote a regular horoscope article which was published in many papers across the country. Two weeks after he moved into the area, the *Weekly Bugle* published his horoscope article and many people commented on how interesting it was. But not everyone. The next week the letters page carried the following letter.

Dear Editor,
I realise that newspapers these days have to find some way of trying to get new customers. However, I wish to object in the strongest possible terms to the *Weekly Bugle* printing superstitious rubbish and treating it as a serious article. I refer, sir, to Mr Armstrong's horoscope column. I really cannot believe that in this scientific day and age, there are still people who believe that the stars affect their lives. We know that these stars are planets, millions and millions of light years away. How could they possibly have any effect on us? I had assumed that we had grown out of such childish beliefs and hope you will drop the column immediately.
Yours faithfully,
Dr Janet Hamilton

Well, that set the cat amongst the pigeons. The *Weekly Bugle*'s post room had never seen anything like it. There were 17 letters over the next few days all about the horoscopes. Mrs Patel had to work overtime to get all the typesetting done and the editor decided to run to an extra page to carry some of the letters. The following week two letters in particular caught people's attention. The first was from Mr Jeremy Armstrong himself.

A Chinese astrologer

Dear Editor,
I wonder if I might be allowed to reply to the worries expressed by Dr Hamilton in her letter last week on horoscopes. I fully appreciate her concern. How indeed can we believe the stars, millions of miles away, affect us? Well, we know that the moon moves the tides, so I do not find the idea of the other planets and the stars having an effect on us strange. But more importantly, Dr Hamilton divides us from the rest of the universe. We know, thanks to science, that all life is energy. This energy cannot be destroyed. We are all part of the energy of life and therefore we are all linked together, whether we know it or not. If I want to walk from my house to the church, I have to go round three bends in the road. I would prefer to walk in a straight line, but nature and

other human beings have made it so that I must go round three bends. That is like life. We have to follow the courses which are set out before us. However, if I was desperate to get to church, I could always take off across the fields. I do have free will, but mostly I am content to follow the path laid out. That is like life. And horoscopes simply tell you the paths or ways that have been prepared. I hope this puts Dr Hamilton's mind at rest.
Yours faithfully,
Jeremy Armstrong

The second letter was from someone who did not wish to give her name. This in itself was most unusual in the *Weekly Bugle*.

Dear Editor,
I am a devout Anglican and attend church most Sundays. I also read horoscopes in the paper and have had my fortune told. I found Armstrong's Horoscopes very helpful. But I wonder if I am doing the right thing? You see, as a Christian I believe in free will. I believe that I can make decisions about what I should do. I look to my faith and my Church to help me in this. There have been a number of times when I have decided whether to do something or not and this has changed my life – like getting married, starting a small business and so on. As a Christian I believe it is important that we take responsibility for our decisions. Then at the same time, I find that certain things seem to happen to me, often at the same times of the year. I cannot explain these 'forces' nor can I seem to have much control over them. This is why I find horoscopes helpful. They don't tell me what to do, no one can! They help me see certain sides of my personality. I am a Libra and I find I always balance things carefully before deciding what to do – just like the scales of Libra. So I would be sorry if Armstrong's Horoscopes were not published in your paper, but I do wonder if I am doing the right thing as a Christian. Please do not give my name or address.
Yours faithfully,
Anonymous

The number of letters in the post bag the next week was over 50, all on the same topic. The ones which captured the most attention were both short and to the point.

Dear Editor,
There is much in this world we do not understand. There are powerful forces which guide us but which we should not try to examine too closely. Through horoscopes, we can be made aware of these forces beyond ourselves. We can be guided to understand why we do what we do. We should be thankful for the wisdom of people like Mr Armstrong.
Yours faithfully,
Amy Hadfield

Dear Editor,
I write as a believing Christian who is proud to be called an evangelical. I want to tell your anonymous Anglican that he/she is wrong and will stand judged by God at the Last Day. No Christian who believes truly in the saving power of Jesus Christ needs horoscopes. Our future lies with God, not with the stars. God, and only God, can direct us to a happy future, so put your trust entirely in God and He will guide your life. Those who play with horoscopes and the dark forces which inhabit this world are in danger of becoming the play things of Satan. The stars have no influence over us, as Dr Hamilton pointed out in her letter – but Satan will use any avenue to trick people away from God.
Yours in Christ,
Mr John Broughton

Information box

Evangelical

This word comes from a Greek word meaning 'good news', or in Christian terms, 'the gospel'. The name 'evangelical' is used by certain groups of Christians who emphasise that their teaching and life are based on what the Bible says, and particularly on the Gospels, the four accounts of Jesus' life in the Bible.

Evangelicals also lay great stress on what they see as the most important 'good news' of all. They say that each person must accept that Jesus died on the cross for him or her, personally. This is all that is needed to gain eternal life, or the kingdom of God. Ceremonies, actions, and living a good life may all follow after this, but they are not as important as this belief.

In the story, Mr John Broughton, who is 'proud to be called an evangelical', would probably point to various passages in the Bible where astrologers, mediums and fortune-tellers are condemned. For example, in Deuteronomy 18: 10–12 it says: 'There must never be anyone among you who . . . practises divination, who is a soothsayer, fortune-teller or sorcerer, who uses charms, consults ghosts or spirits, or calls up the dead. For the man who does these things is detestable to the Lord your God.'

In the New Testament, astrology and fortune-telling are not mentioned much, but in the Acts of the Apostles there is a story of a girl who used to tell fortunes but could no longer do so when Paul spoke to her in the name of Jesus. This can be found in Acts 16: 16–18.

Activities

1. Continue the correspondence by writing a letter from any of the following kinds of people:
   - the local vicar; the head of the local school; a Hindu living in the area
   - a reply from Mr Armstrong; a reply from Dr Hamilton; a scientist; an astronomer (note that astronomers are not the same as astrologers!)
   - a comment from the editor explaining either his reasons for keeping the column in his paper or his reasons for dropping it.
2. Look at horoscopes in your local paper and find out from the newspaper why it publishes them.

The Disturbance

The Wilkinsons had not been in the house long when it started. At first it was Jessica, the 13-year-old daughter, who noticed something strange. She was a very tidy person. Every night she put out the clothes for the next day on the chair by her bed. On the second day they were in the house, she awoke to find all her clothes thrown on the floor. She thought she must have knocked them off in the night. So the next night she carefully put the chair away from her bed and put her clothes out. The next morning they were all thrown on the floor again.

Jessica told her mother who told her not to worry, it was perhaps the wind or something like that. But then Terry, Jessica's 15-year-old brother, found things went missing. He liked taking computers apart and rebuilding them. A few days after they arrived, he spread all his bits and pieces out ready to start work the next day. In the morning, half the pieces were missing and he found them scattered around the house. He blamed it on Fran, his little sister, who, being eight and very cheeky, was quite likely to do such things. But his dad pointed out that Fran had been asleep long before Terry had gone to bed.

The family began to feel a little scared. They asked a neighbour if the previous owners had seen unusual things happen. But the neighbour said it was the first that he had heard about it.

It was about two weeks later that things became very bad. Objects were being moved, disappearing and then turning up in odd places. The family became more and more worried. Then, one night, Mr and Mrs Wilkinson were watching TV when suddenly the central light in the room went out.

'Blast,' said Mrs Wilkinson, and got up to fetch a new bulb. The glow from the TV meant she could see the wall switch quite clearly. When the light bulb flickered on, then off, then on again, her husband thought it was simply an electrical fault such as a loose connection. But then Mrs Wilkinson screamed and fainted. When she came round, all the family were gathered around her.

'What happened, Mum?' asked Jessica.

'What did you see, dear?' asked her husband.

For a few moments she found it impossible to speak. Then she said, 'The light switch! I saw it move! There was nothing wrong with the bulb – it was just being switched on and off. And nobody was doing it!'

A few minutes later the telephone rang at the vicarage. The Revd Nigel Brown answered just as he was getting ready for bed. Mr Wilkinson explained what had happened.

'Could you possibly come round now? he pleaded. 'We daren't go to bed.'

'I'll come, of course,' said Nigel Brown, 'but I've no training in dealing with ghosts or anything like that. I'll do what I can tonight and tomorrow I'll contact someone who knows more about it – our diocese has a person who deals with this sort of thing.'

After the vicar had been, the family were a little more relaxed. He had helped them all pray by saying the Psalm 23, which was very calming. He had prayed for them that they would spend a quiet night. But none of them slept well.

The next day, the vicar returned with another clergyman, Revd Arthur Thomas.

'Are you the exorcist?' asked Jessica.

'Well, we don't usually use that word. Jesus gave his disciples authority over all the things that trouble people – illness, depression, unfriendly spirits, or whatever it might be. In Jesus' name, by prayer, people can be set free from them. That's why we call it "the ministry of deliverance". Most local vicars don't have much experience with the sort of trouble you've been having, so they call me in for advice.'

'Oh, so you do believe I didn't imagine what I saw?' said Mrs Wilkinson, 'I don't think the vicar did. He seemed to think that we had all just got too worked up, and that's what made it happen.'

'Oh, no, these things are real, all right. None of us quite understands them, but God does, and he can protect us from them if we ask him to. I'd like to pray and talk with you for a while.'

It took quite a while, and Arthur Thomas found out quite a lot about the family and the house, and what had been happening. He prayed with each one of them. Then he prayed for God's blessing and protection on each room in the house, and in Jesus' name he commanded the spirit that was bothering them to depart and not to trouble them any more. Gradually he helped the Wilkinsons realise that they had nothing to fear. And from that day on, the Wilkinsons' house was like any other – except that Mrs Wilkinson did not like to be alone in the front room.

Information box

Exorcism

Exorcism is the practice of expelling unhappy or evil spirits from a place or a person by means of prayer or set formulas.

Since the time of the New Testament, the Christian Church has followed Christ's example and exorcised people or places possessed of these spirits. Sometimes, however, a priest will carry out an exorcism, not because a person is possessed, but to protect him or her from the evil forces.

Jesus driving the devils out in to the pigs

Exorcism *continued*

There is a story in the New Testament of a man who was possessed by such violent spirits that nobody dared to go near him. He was continually naked and lived amongst the tombs scattered on a hillside outside a town. Jesus approached him fearlessly and through his unconditional love for the mad man the evil spirits were driven out of the mad man and entered a herd of pigs grazing on a nearby hill. The force of the spirits drove the pigs over the edge of the hill and into a lake where they drowned. From that day the man lived normally and peacefully.

You can read this account in Mark 5, Luke 8 and Matthew 8.

Activities

1. Nigel Brown, the local vicar, seemed to think that the Wilkinsons had imagined that things were happening in their house. What explanations might he have given for what was going on? Do you agree with him?
2. Work in pairs to write a conversation between Jessica or Terry and a friend, about what has happened in the Wilkinsons' house. Plan first how each person reacts. Is Jessica frightened, annoyed, puzzled, excited? Is the friend frightened, interested, disbelieving, calming? Does either of them change his or her attitude in the course of the conversation?
3. There are many passages in the Bible encouraging people to trust in God and not be afraid. One of these is mentioned in the story, when the vicar read Psalm 23 with the Wilkinson family. Here are some others:
   Psalm 27: 1
   Psalm 56: 3–4
   Proverbs 18: 10
   Isaiah 12: 2
   Isaiah 41: 10
   John 14: 27
   Romans 8: 38–9.

   Look up some of these passages (share them out between you so that the class looks up all of them). Choose one or two verses that you think the Revd Arthur Thomas might have suggested to the Wilkinson family to calm their fears. Write out your chosen verses in a way that the Wilkinsons might like to have framed, perhaps with a picture or suitable pattern.

Sources

BUDDHISM

The Buddha was very down-to-earth in response to questions and speculations about 'the unknown', life after death and similar matters. He believed that such questions simply divert our attention away from the greatest of all 'unknowns' – why is there suffering and unhappiness in life and how can we liberate ourselves from them?

The Buddha told the following story to illustrate how some questions can distract us from what is important:

> Imagine a man who is struck by a poisoned arrow. His friends rush him to a surgeon, but the surgeon says, "I will not let this arrow be removed until I know who shot it, where he

Buddhism *continued*

comes from, whether he is tall or short, dark or fair skinned. And I must know what kind of bow was used, the type of arrow, the kind of feather used on the arrow, and with what the arrow was tipped." The injured man would surely die before the surgeon could know any of these things. The same applies to those who, instead of dedicating themselves to discovering the meaning of their lives, waste time with questions about who created the universe and similar speculations.

In Buddhism there is nothing very special about spirits and other disembodied beings, who can be just as ignorant and deluded as beings with bodies such as you and me! Psychic forces are no more than subtle energy, like the vital energy which, Buddhists believe, carries through to another rebirth after our death. It is not our self, our personality or our 'soul' that is reborn, although it is possible to recall past lives.

CHRISTIANITY

There are two different senses in which the unknown is understood in Christianity. First of all there is the fact that God is unknowable. The early writers of the Church, known as the Church Fathers, were very clear on this. While God had revealed much about himself in the person of Jesus Christ and through the prophets, this did not mean that we knew or ever could know all about God. Clement of Alexandria said that God is beyond place, time, description and understanding. This is an important teaching because some people were claiming that they could know God completely and thus become God.

The second understanding of the unknown in Christianity refers to the existence of realms and 'worlds' which are unknown to us. In classical Christian theology, there is a whole world of the angels, of the blessed, of the Communion of Saints, which is beyond our knowledge at this time. Thus the Creed says 'We believe in one God, the Father Almighty, maker of Heaven and Earth and of all things visible and invisible.' The last part stresses that there is more to the universe than we can ever know, even if we can count all the stars!

But Christianity also teaches that there are some ways of trying to gain knowledge or power, such as trying to contact the spirits of the dead, which are wrong.

HINDUISM

The area of the unknown is treated seriously in the Hindu religion and receives a lot of attention. The existence of ghosts is considered to be a proven fact and there are thought to be different types of ghosts - good, bad, powerful ones and so on. If someone commits suicide or becomes distanced from everyday life, for example, by taking drugs or excessive alcohol to the extent that they cannot cope with physical existence, then they become a ghost. In addition, if a person was very attached to a particular place in their previous identity they may become a ghost and haunt this place.

Some Hindu priests are capable of exorcising ghosts. In India you often see a straw figure outside a new construction site. The priest performs a ceremony at the construction site which obliges all the ghosts to enter into the straw figure which is then burned.

The signs of the zodiac and the whole science of the horoscope is found in ancient Hindu scriptures and is part of Hindu culture. The horoscope is used on different occasions such as the time of an arranged marriage or the birth of a baby. Before a marriage is agreed, horoscope readings are taken to see if the partners are compatible, and if they are, the horoscope is used to find a suitable day to marry. When a baby is born the parents make a note of the time and place of birth so that the child's horoscope can be read at important times in his or her life.

JUDAISM

In the days before modern science Jews took an active interest in many aspects of the unknown. Many Jews, including rabbis, believed in astrology, although some held that the stars could have no influence over Jews, who were under the direct influence of God. Traces of this belief can still be found in words used by Jews, notably the expression 'mazzal tov', literally 'a good star'.

Even when the belief in astrology was strong, however, it was taught that the Jew should leave the future to God and not consult astrologers or cast lots to determine the future.

There are two reasons why a belief in astrology lost its respectability in modern times. First, the use of scientific method made astrology increasingly improbable, as it cannot be shown that a person's life is influenced by the stars under which they were born. Secondly, astrological systems are based on the assumption that the earth is at the centre of the universe, with the spheres, containing the stars and planets, revolving around it. Modern astronomy has shown that the universe is not centred on the earth. Before the rise of modern science, astrology did seem to be convincing to educated and sophisticated people.

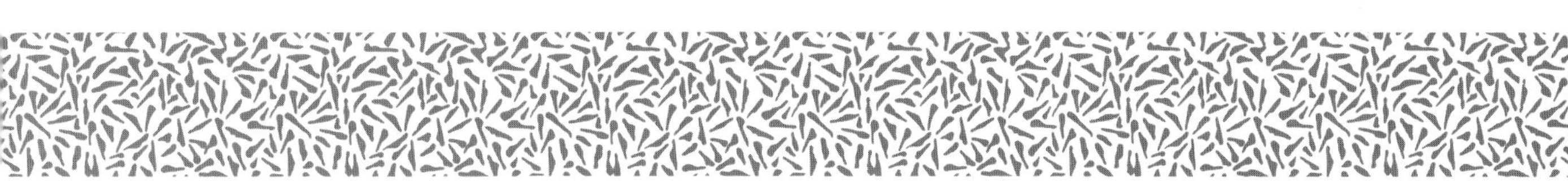

1. It is quite easy to be frightened or misled into thinking something is unknown or mysterious simply because we do not understand it. For instance, one of the writers of this book was once staying in an old wooden house when he was a child. The first night he went to bed he awoke at about midnight. He was convinced that someone was walking around his room. The floorboards creaked as if someone was walking on them. Yet there was nobody there. He spent the night shivering with fear even after the noises had stopped. The next morning he discovered it was simply the floorboards creaking as the central heating went off!

The first task we want you to try is quite simple. In groups, take a very ordinary object such as a loaf of bread or a cup, for example. Then write a description of it which is true, but mysterious. For example, you might describe a loaf of bread as 'a strange material which rises as if it was alive and unless you kill it with fire, it will spread everywhere. Once it has been heated it can be eaten!' Try to find a strange or mysterious way of describing objects like a door, a light switch, a TV, an oven, an automatic kettle . . . !

Once you have your descriptions, read them to the rest of the class and see if they can guess your object. You will find it is quite easy to make the most innocent thing sound sinister!

2. But there is still the area of the genuinely 'unknown'. The 'unknown' can be things 'out there' – ghosts, spirits, the power and love of God – and so on. But it can also be within us.

There are times when something inside us seems to take over. It might be anger, or sadness, or love. There is much about ourselves which we do not know. It is not easy to explore things like this in class. However, try the following role-play situations and see what you make of them.

a) The school is apparently being haunted by a ghost. It appears to be the ghost of a former pupil who was very unhappy here. It is seen weeping in corners and then disappears into the walls. The school is very divided over what to do. The key characters are the following:

- the head teacher, who does not believe in ghosts but realises that the school is becoming very upset over the supposed sighting
- the head of the lower school, Mr Patel, who is a Hindu

- the head of the upper school, Mrs Green, who is a Christian
- the local school inspector, who is an atheist.

A meeting is called at which all these people are present. What would each person have to say and what sort of plan would emerge from such a group?

b) You are running a charity fair one summer. You have always had a gipsy fortune-teller's tent. This year however, some people have objected to you having a fortune-teller. Split into two groups. One group has to argue against having the fortune-teller, the other group, for having the fortune-teller.

THE SACRED

Space

'You don't mind sharing your room do you? It'll only be for ten days. After all, your cousin doesn't often come, does he?'

This was the first Joseph knew of the forthcoming visit of his uncle, aunt and cousin, Alan. They lived in Canada and visited England once every five or six years. Joseph could not even remember the last time he had seen them.

'Isn't it wonderful that they will be with us for Passover?' continued his mother. Naturally, she was excited at the idea of seeing her brother. 'We can all be one big family together.'

Joseph looked at his younger sister, Esther. She did not seem to be bothered either way. But Joseph felt angry.

'Why my room?' he asked. 'There isn't much space you know.' He wanted to add 'and it's my room, so I say who uses it', but decided not to be aggressive.

'Now don't be selfish,' said Joseph's father. 'It's not for long and I'm sure you will get on very well with Alan.'

So it was all arranged. And Joseph even managed to convince himself that he did not really mind. Then his relatives arrived. Joseph had never understood why people always talk about 'friends and relations' as if it was impossible to have any relatives who were also your friends. With the arrival of his uncle, aunt and their youngest son Alan, he began to see why people felt that way!

Joseph loved Passover. It was always a time of great preparations, such as cleaning the house and planning for the Passover Meal. The service in the synagogue and all the special rituals at home always made him feel proud to be Jewish.

Passover this year, however, was a disaster. First of all, his aunt seemed to annoy his mother. His aunt was always trying to tidy up as if she was in her own house! Then there was the problem of Alan. When Alan moved into Joseph's room, Joseph was very polite. He gave Alan three drawers in his cupboard and space in his wardrobe. But within a day, Alan had spread his belongings all over the room. Then came the argument about the model ship. Joseph had a model ship made of balsa wood on his desk. He had made it in Year 5 and it had won him a prize. He loved the model and took great care of it. On the fourth night, Alan finished reading his book and threw it carelessly on to the desk.

It skidded across the desk and smacked into the model, breaking the masts.

'Look what you've done!' cried Joseph.

'It's only a toy, what's the fuss?' replied Alan.

Joseph became very angry. Alan had invaded his space, his room and now had broken something very special. All his pent-up frustration erupted. It took both his uncle and his mother to separate the two of them. Alan was moved out into the living room and an atmosphere of hostility settled over the house. Joseph's mother took him aside.

'What was all that about?' she asked. So he told her how angry he was at having his room treated like that. 'I know,' said his mother. 'I feel like that about the way your aunt behaves. But we've got to try to be more friendly. It's hard for our visitors. They don't feel comfortable because we have to fit them in. So let's both be a bit more understanding, shall we?'

The final straw came when they all went to synagogue. 'What's all that scaffolding doing beside the Ark?' demanded Joseph, for rising up at the front of the synagogue was an ugly scaffold.

'We've got a bad leak in the roof and we've found wet rot,' said one of the stewards. 'If we don't get the plaster off now, it could lead to serious problems.'

Joseph found this too much. Not only was his home crowded and he was sharing his room again with Alan and his things, but now the synagogue was invaded. 'Is nowhere sacred?' he wondered angrily.

Later that day, Joseph slipped out of the crowded, disrupted house. He went down to the local park. There he found his old sitting place. When he was younger he had found a natural den. Two trees grew very close together in front of an old high wall. If you climbed the trees, you could sit on the wall and watch the world go by and no one knew you were there. Here, at last, he found some peace.

He sat for a long time, thinking. He thought about his room, his special things, about the synagogue and the scaffolding around the Ark.

'I bet Passover night will be terrible,' he thought.

The room was more crowded than ever and there was only just enough space on the table for all the plates and Haggadah books. Joseph was uncomfortable, and hardly said anything as the family began their celebrations. During the meal he began to relax and after the meal, as the family sang their favourite Passover songs, Joseph finally realised that his worries had disappeared. As the singing became louder and louder, he had that happy feeling he always had when he shared Passover with his family. Looking around the crowded table he felt he was amongst people who, despite everything, were both family and friends.

Information box

Passover

Passover, which lasts eight days, is the time to recall the deliverance of the Jewish people from slavery in the land of Egypt. After years of hardship and persecution in Egypt the Jews were ordered out by the Pharaoh. The Jews were hurriedly gathered together by Moses and they only had time to eat the lamb they had killed and to make

bread before they made their escape. The bread did not have time to rise. During their Exodus from Egypt the Jews faced many hardships: it took 40 years of wandering to reach their destination. In times of hardship God would always help them and thereby showed the Jewish people that He was their God and that they were His chosen people. During the Passover Jews retell the story of the Exodus, and the food and drink that they share is in remembrance of their journey out of Egypt and of their sufferings.

Activities

1. There are many examples of activities that some people feel would be unsuitable for certain places: for example, a pop concert at Lord's cricket ground; dancing in a library; a picnic in a graveyard. Make a list of other examples. Then take one example and explain:

   - why some people might think it is unsuitable
   - why some people might think it is alright.

   Explain which view you agree with.
2. Many victims of burglary are deeply upset by the thought that a stranger has rummaged through their personal things, even if nothing of value has been taken. Imagine you are in this situation, and write a letter to your best friend, explaining how you feel.
3. Draw a picture with the caption 'But you can't do that here!' Or make a play that includes those words.
4. What is the most peaceful place you know? Describe it in words, music or pictures. Compare your 'peaceful place' with those of others, and discuss these points:
   - What makes it peaceful?
   - How did it come to be?
   - Does anyone look after it?
   - What might threaten its peace?
   - How can it be preserved as a peaceful place?
   - Do any creatures other than humans benefit from it?

Sanctuary

Roger had been an apprentice at the silversmith's for nearly four years. After three more years he would be a qualified silversmith. But as Roger worked on his own in the shop, he wondered whether he would manage to stay on for those three years.

When he had first come to the shop, in Silver Row, the old master had been alive. He was a kindly man, skilful with his hands, and he could make the most beautiful decorations. He had been kind to Roger and had taught him well. But then the old master died and the young master, Arnold, returned from the south.

'He's no good,' said Roger to himself as he heated some silver on a brazier of red-hot charcoal. 'No good for me or the business. He doesn't love the silver the way the old master did, and I can do the work better than he can. He only wants the silver for its money value – and the way he's spending, I don't think it's going to last much longer.'

It was the first full working day after St Martin's Day, just as autumn passed into winter, that Arnold burst into the shop after a long morning of drinking with his friends.

'There he is!' shouted Arnold, pointing at Roger. 'There's the thief. Grab him!'

Roger could not believe his ears.

'What do you mean, master?' he asked.

'Don't come the innocent one with me, my boy,' said Arnold. 'I know that you have been stealing my silver. That's why there's no money left. To think my poor father trusted you. I went to pay

the bills yesterday and found the money chest empty.'

Roger was about to protest that if anyone had emptied the chest it was Arnold. But he looked at the threatening figures of Arnold's four companions and he decided that it was not the time for such a discussion. With a quick flip of his hands, he threw the red-hot brazier towards Arnold and his friends. While they hopped about dodging fiery coals, Roger dived out of the back door and began to run.

As he stumbled desperately up the lane behind the shop, he could hear Arnold and his friends shouting behind him. He had to find somewhere where he could think! Somewhere safe where he could tell people that he was not a thief and that it was all lies!

As he turned one corner, he saw in the distance the cross on the top of St Leonard's church. With a gasp of relief, he ran on to the church. He was only just in time, for close behind him came Arnold and his four friends. They drew closer and closer, and Roger thought his lungs would burst before he reached safety. With a final desperate effort Roger threw himself through the church door and ran to the altar. He clung to it, panting and sobbing.

The four friends stopped as they came into the church.

'Come on!' roared Arnold, 'Let's get him now!'

But his friends would not follow.

'Not in a church!' said one.

'He's got sanctuary now, leave him be,' said another.

Arnold shook his head in anger and turned to stride forward to the altar. God alone knows what might have happened if the parish priest had not hurried in.

'Father!' cried Roger, 'I am claiming sanctuary and the protection of Mother Church!'

'What has happened, my son?' asked the priest. 'Are you innocent of any crime?'

'I am, Father, I swear it!' cried Roger, 'Save me from this man!'

'He's a thief!' roared Arnold, 'Just let me drag him out to the punishment he deserves!'

'The law will punish him, all in good time,' said the priest, 'If, that is, you can prove what you say about him is true. You will both get your chance to speak. Now go, and do not profane this holy place any more, or you will suffer God's anger!'

As Arnold and his companions left, Roger collapsed with exhaustion. The priest brought him food and wine, and explained that he must stay where he was. The church would take care of him and no one could harm him.

Ten days later, before the town judge and the bishop, the case was tried. Arnold tried very hard to present a case against Roger, but it soon fell apart. Too many people had noticed the way Arnold was spending money and too many people knew Roger as a trustworthy young man. Arnold was found guilty and branded on his forehead as a sign of shame. Roger was found innocent.

In later years Roger became a wealthy silversmith, and as soon as he could, he presented the church of St Leonard with a pair of beautiful silver candlesticks in thanks for the sanctuary which the church had given him.

'But for this sacred place,' he said, 'I could have been killed.'

Information box

Sanctuary

The word sanctuary comes from the Latin word sanctus meaning 'holy'. The holiest part of a church or temple is called a sanctuary and some holy sites are also called sanctuaries. It is also possible to 'seek sanctuary', which means to look for a place of safety.

In the Middle Ages, there was a commonly recognised right of sanctuary within certain churches. Any person, criminal or not, who claimed sanctuary, was given it. In some churches they had to touch a specific object, such as the sanctuary knocker on the door of Durham Cathedral, but most commonly it was the altar.

Sanctuary knocker at Durham Cathedral

Once sanctuary had been claimed, the person involved had 40 days in which either to answer the charge, or, if guilty, to accept the offer by the church of safe passage to a sea port where they could leave the country. However, this could only be done after swearing an oath never to commit an offence again. The right of sanctuary was abolished in the UK in 1623 for those who had committed a crime.

The word sanctuary is also used in a much wider sense to imply a place of safety from danger or persecution.

Wildlife sanctuary in Nigeria

Refugees escaping war may find sanctuary in an embassy or another country, or animals and birds may find sanctuary in a nature reserve. Animal hospitals that have been set up to care for abused and sick animals are called sanctuaries, since they are places of protection and care.

Activities

1. How could Roger be sure he was safe in the church? Was it because the church was well-protected and locked against intruders, or for some other reason?
2. Is there a safe place in your school? Imagine you were advising a younger brother or sister how to avoid bullies. You know you cannot watch over them all the time, so where would you advise them to run to if they are in danger? What makes this place safe?
3. Look for newspaper or television reports, advertisements, appeals, etc., which show people either looking for, or offering sanctuary. The reports might use other words such as 'asylum', 'refuge', or 'reserve'.
   - Who or what is seeking safety?
   - What is the danger?
   - How are they being protected?

Sources

CHRISTIANITY

The idea of the sacred is very strong within much of Roman Catholic and Orthodox Christianity. The term is used to describe those places such as altars or shrines, and objects such as holy icons, blessed bread and wine or relics of the saints, which are felt to be filled with a special power. In Orthodox churches, only priests are allowed into the area of the altar. This area is sacred because Orthodoxy teaches that heaven and earth meet at the altar. The altar area is screened by the wall of icons called an iconostasis. This emphasises the sacred nature of the area.

In Roman Catholicism saints' relics are sacred because they carry something of the power of the actual saint. Likewise, sanctified bread and wine for the Communion service is considered sacred and is treated with great respect.

However, not all Christians share this idea of the sacred. Many Protestant groups see only the Bible as sacred. The Quakers go even further. Quakers believe that there is no split between religion and daily life. Therefore there are no times, or places, or people that are seen as being more sacred than others. Quakers believe there is no need for any specific person to be designated prophet, priest or church leader. They say if people are open to the power of love and light in their lives then they will themselves become prophetic and priestly, and will not need to follow the external authority of church leaders. They will have the strength to be at peace with themselves, to find God in their heart and to serve other people.

No one in the Quaker community has a 'holier' function than anyone else and in the same way no times or seasons of the year are regarded as being more holy than others. The early Quakers rejected Christmas and Easter because they believed that Christ's birth, death and resurrection were ever present in their hearts. It was for this reason that many Quakers kept their shops open on established religious festivals. In the eyes of others this was sometimes seen as a clever way of making more money. Quakers still believe that all time is sacred, although some do hold special meetings for worship at Christmas and Easter.

Many Quakers worship on Sunday morning in a Friends' Meeting House, but this is for convenience, not because Sunday is holier than the rest of the week. Some Quakers do not have a meeting place at all – they meet in church halls, each other's houses or even outside in the open air.

DUWAMISH INDIANS

For many indigenous cultures, the natural world and the land is seen as being sacred.

Over a century ago most of the land which is now called the state of Washington was the home of Duwamish, a tribe of native people – 'Red Indians' – who had lived there for more than a thousand years. In 1854, the Chief of the Duwamish, Chief Seattle, delivered a speech to his people in which he talked about the coming of the 'white man' and of the differences between his culture and that of the new settlers with their alien understanding of land ownership:

> How can you buy or sell the sky, the warmth of the land? This idea is strange to us. If we do not own the freshness of the air and the sparkle of the water, how can you buy them? Every part of this earth is sacred to my people. Every shining pine needle, every sandy shore, every mist in the dark woods, every clearing and humming insect is holy in the memory and experience of my people.

HINDUISM

Place: A place is sacred in Hindu culture if the souls of those who are dead are present or if there is the presence of a divine being in one of the many forms they are capable of taking. This is why temples are sacred places and the image of a particular deity is stored in each temple. Through worship of the image the deity is attracted to the temple and then becomes present. A Hindu's visit to a sacred place is a very important act and this will usually be done every day.

Time: In Hindu culture the day is divided into muhurtas; the Brahmamurta is the period of time which occurs just before dawn, and that is the time that all religious people will perform their worship. There are also holy days and sacred days such as the Dark Moon (or New Moon) Night. The four months of the rainy season (roughly from July to October) are seen as a period for spiritual practice.

Role-play

1. Canterbury Cathedral is a very special and sacred place. It was here that St Augustine first re-established Christianity in southern Britain in the sixth century. In Canterbury, the cathedral stands not only as a beautiful cathedral, but as the mother church of the Anglican Church in the UK and worldwide. It is a place where saints have lived and died and for centuries pilgrims from all around the world have come here.

   Around the cathedral itself are the Precincts. Beautiful old houses and lawns are to be found there along with the Archbishop's Palace. Here, the powerful figures of the church live and a famous private school has its buildings and grounds. Here, people come to find peace and quiet, and sometimes to pause in their busy lives to think about God.

   But some people feel this is not how a Christian sacred place should be. They want to see the private school and the clergy turned out of their comfortable houses and the buildings used to look after those whom Jesus most cared for – the sick, the poor and the homeless. It has been suggested that an AIDS hostel be set up in part of the Archbishop's Palace; that a hostel for the homeless be put in one of the old houses and a special home for old people who need Christian love to care for them. People argue that this would make the Precinct a more sacred place, because it would be doing the work Christ came to do.

   On the next page is a map of the precincts of Canterbury Cathedral. How would you use this place to show what is special to Christianity?

2. The following passage appeared in *Religion for a Change* Book One:

   Imagine an ancient tribe and their religion. The centre of all their ceremonies is the sacred cave which runs under the nearby mountain. The entrance of the cave is half-way up the mountain. It can be seen from the village, but the path to it is steep and dangerous. Deep inside the mountain, the cave opens wider into a cavern. From the high ceiling, a drop of water falls every few seconds into the pool beneath. The pool stays the same size all the time – as the water drips in, so it slowly seeps away below. It is said that if the pool ever dries up or overflows, the life of the tribe will end. Every day, one man or woman climbs up the steep path to the cave, goes inside and lets one drop of blood from their thumb fall into

the pool. All adults take their turn to do this, and as their turn comes round, about once a year, they look forward eagerly to the honour of helping to keep the tribe alive.

Now imagine that time has moved on, and the tribe has been discovered by the producer of a television documentary programme. She wants to bring a camera crew to film the ceremony. But up to now the ceremony has always been performed by each person totally alone, with no one watching.

One group of you are villagers who feel that to let anyone film the ceremony would be wrong. Another group feel that their religion is something of value and interest, and that it would be good to let the outside world see their ceremony, provided it was done with respect. The producer and her team want to persuade the villagers to let them film, and they want to cause as little offence as possible. They try to think of ways that the ceremony could be filmed without upsetting anyone.

A meeting is arranged for all the villagers with the producer and her team. Each group should prepare its arguments carefully beforehand, and then meet to explain its feelings and discuss the problem.

DRUGS AND ALCOHOL

International Drug Dealers

It had all started some six years previously. Suzanne was the only daughter of a wealthy English businessman and his wife in Hong Kong. She could see now that she had been spoilt. Hong Kong is a great place to be if you have money and she had plenty of that. But after a while she had got bored. She began to take drugs as a joke. Soon the joke got out of control. Her father and mother had tried everything to help her, but in one way they were actually part of the problem.

The final point came, in all places, in the drugs club she went to in the worst area of Hong Kong – the famous Walled City. For all sorts of reasons, this part of Hong Kong was a safe haven for criminals. The apartments here are small and tightly packed. Little light comes into the dark, narrow alleyways that twist through the city. Many of the open drains lead on to the street and rubbish is piled high in doorways. The people who live here are poor and many are involved in drug trafficking, drug taking or gang violence. One night when Suzanne was lost and dazed from taking too many drugs, she wandered into the Walled City. She wandered into a small, brightly lit room full of people. It was here that she met Jackie Pullinger. Jackie is a Christian who runs programmes to help young people, Chinese and non-Chinese, who are addicted to drugs. She also works with the criminals, and over the years she has been there she has helped many to escape from both crime and drugs. She found Suzanne and brought her to a living faith in Jesus Christ. In tears one night, Suzanne opened her heart and poured out all her sorrows. She felt the power and love of Jesus come into her life and she realised she had to live without drugs, for his sake as well as her own.

It was harder than she had ever believed possible, but slowly the terrible dreams and the awful pain in her head and stomach began to fade. She could now hold a cup without spilling it. Her eyesight was getting better and the feeling of nausea was easing. The experience had been frightening beyond belief, but luckily belief had been what had helped her.

As she began to recover, she became good friends with a Chinese woman, Wai Ming. One day she commented to Wai Ming that there had always been a drug problem in China. 'People used to smoke opium all day, didn't they?' she said. Wai Ming reacted angrily.

'How dare you,' she said. 'Do you have any idea of what the British did to my people?' Suzanne shook her head, silenced by Wai Ming's anger.

'The Chinese knew about opium long before the Western world found out about it. I've read in books that it was used by our doctors to help people in pain. A little helps to take away pain. After all, people all round the world have known about drugs for thousands of years. I believe that in America, some of the native people use drugs in their religious ceremonies and it doesn't harm them.

'The British started trading with China. They were surprised that the Chinese didn't seem to want to buy much from them. However, there was one thing some people wanted. Someone had discovered that if you smoked opium it did more than just relieve your pain. It gave you a high. At first, very few people smoked opium. It was too expensive. But then the British began to smuggle opium to China. Our government, the Emperors themselves, tried to stop them. It was illegal. But the British and then the other European nations as well, continued to smuggle opium. The British grew the opium in India and then shipped it to China.'

'If people were buying it they must have wanted it, so what's wrong with that?' queried Suzanne.

'Oh yes, people wanted it, but if the British hadn't smuggled so much, then not so many people would have become addicted. I read somewhere that at the height of the trade, around 1830, nine out of ten adults in the areas around Kwangtung were addicts. The opium was killing Chinese people.'

'But surely,' replied Suzanne, 'your government could put a stop to it?'

'They tried,' replied Wai Ming. 'The Emperor published laws forbidding the trade. But of course a lot of Chinese officials were making money from the trade. There was a lot of corruption among the government officials. Then the Emperor appointed the great Commissioner Lin. He was a good man. Honest and fearless. In 1839 he seized all the opium he could find – from the British ships, factories and other places. And he burned it. Now don't forget, this was illegal opium. But the British declared war on China and using her superior military power, defeated China and demanded the right to sell opium! Britain also took Hong Kong at the same time.'

'I don't believe you!' cried Suzanne, near to tears. It can't be true!'

'I'm sorry,' said Wai Ming, 'I shouldn't have shouted at you. It's not your fault. But British people just don't know what went on and it really makes me angry. But you read a few history books and you'll see that what I told you is true.

So Suzanne did, and that was how the full impact of the story hit her. She discovered that the company her father worked for had originally made its money in the illegal opium trade!

Lithograph of the Opium Wars

Activities

1. Why do you think the story says that Suzanne's mother and father were, in a way, part of the problem?

2. Who do you think is most to blame for drug addiction:
   - foolish people who experiment with drugs
   - drug dealers
   - governments who do not put enough effort into controlling the trade in drugs
   - governments who crack down and send the whole trade 'underground'
   - parents who do not take enough care of their children
   - any other people or agencies you think are responsible? Say who you think they are.

   If you think the blame should lie with several of these, draw a pie chart showing how you would share out the blame.

3. Conduct a survey based on the question above. Perhaps you could turn it into a series of statements to agree or disagree with. Conduct the survey in school first, and then ask other groups of people to answer the questions, for example, parents, local churches or other religious groups, residents of a drug rehabilitation centre if there is one near you. You would have to take care that people could answer confidentially.

4. There are many reasons which contribute to a person becoming a drug addict. Some are to do with other people and some are to do with personal circumstances.

   Most people think they can say 'no' to drugs – but it is not always so easy. Below are some situations which people find themselves in. Try to work out what each person might say to avoid taking drugs. Are there any situations you can think of and responses you would make?
   - You have just made friends with a new group and want to impress them. At your first party with them, they are offering drugs.
   - Your boyfriend/girlfriend offers you drugs and calls you a coward for refusing.
   - You are very depressed and feel you 'need' drugs to help you get by.
   - You want to win a sports fixture. You are offered drugs at the gym to help improve your performance.

5. For some people, life seems so hard that drugs seem to be a solution to loneliness, pain, sadness, depression or boredom. Take two such feelings and try to work out what you would do, not using drugs or alcohol, to get yourself out of those feelings.

The Ad

Michelle could tell something was up as soon as she came into the Hall. She had been coming to the Drama Club for the last two years. They met twice a week and every night when they were putting on a show. No one, except Pete, was over 21. When you reached 21, you had to leave – except Pete, of course. Pete was the Director and it had been his idea to set up a young people's drama club. It was very popular and there was a waiting list of people wanting to join.

But tonight, there was even more than the usual excitement. Almost everyone was there and they all gathered round Pete.

'Ah, Michelle – good,' said Pete, as Michelle came into the club. 'Now, let's just wait for Bob and Diane and then I'll tell you what this says,' he said, waving a letter from the local TV station in the air.

By the time Bob and Diane arrived the group was on tenterhooks. 'No prizes for guessing why they were late,' thought Michelle.

'Right,' said Pete, 'Trident TV have written to us. They want to make an advertisement for TV about the dangers of drugs and alcohol. Apparently they have decided it should be made by young people. So, they have asked if we will meet them, script an advertisement and then act it out while they film. Do you think I should agree?'

The cheer nearly took the roof off!

Two weeks later, they all met again. This time the Head of Programme Planning from Trident TV was there, Mike Small, and the Director of Public Information section, Tony Burt.

'Right,' said Mike Small, 'I'd like to hear what ideas you've come up with. Remember, we have to get over to people your age why messing around with drink and with drugs is so dangerous. So let's hear what thoughts you've got.'

Adrian spoke up first. 'I thought we could open with these people in a bar, drinking. Then in come three men offering to sell them all drugs. The people in the bar refuse to buy them, so the three men pull out machine guns and kill them!'

You could almost hear the groan from the others and Michelle saw Pete raise his eyes to the ceiling. But Tony Burt proved to be a true diplomat.

'That's got action in it – but maybe it's just a bit too fast for your average viewer. But I like your sense of the dramatic.'

It was Cherry's turn next. 'I think we should try to show how someone's life is ruined by either drink or drugs. What I think would be good are two friends who go to school together. One starts drinking. The other tries to stop her. But it's no good. The drinking friend becomes violent and does badly at school. Eventually she gets into a terrible accident because she is drunk. In hospital her friend comes to see her and they work out how to get her off alcohol.'

'I like a lot in that idea,' said Mike Small, 'but there's a bit of the message I don't think is so good. It sounds like you're saying any drinking is bad. Now I like a pint of beer and I usually have a glass of wine at supper. I'm not about to fall under a bus, am I?'

Everyone laughed at that, including Cherry.

The next person was Diane, who for once was not arm in arm with Bob. There was a rumour that they had had a big row.

'I think we should look at some of the reasons why people take drugs or get drunk. What about opening with someone who's just broken up with his girlfriend and who is feeling lost and upset? He turns to drugs to try to heal the pain. This leads him into needing more and more drugs and more and more money. We see his physical appearance change and he gets involved in petty crime. Eventually, he tries to mug his old girlfriend but she recognises him, calls out his name and he suddenly sees where this has brought him to.'

'Very good,' said Tony Burt. 'Good storyline – not too heavy in its message – though I think we may need to rethink the ending.'

Next came Muhammad who was a good actor and a very devout Muslim. He had to argue with his imam, the teacher at his mosque, to be allowed to join the church Drama Club but as it was the only young people's drama club in the city, he had won the argument.

'You made a good point about not regarding drinking as unusual,' he said to Mike. 'I don't drink because the Qur'an says it is wrong, but neither do I condemn my friends who do – so long as they don't run risks. Nor would I ever take drugs. I've two friends who do, because life is tough for one and too easy for the other. But I argue with them. Is there some way we can show that people like me, while not drinking, can understand a proper use of drink, but that we can never accept the use of drugs?'

There was a long pause before Mike said, 'That's a very major point you've made there. Sorry if I seemed a bit flippant – it wasn't meant that way. I'm not sure how we move on from here.'

This was when Michelle spoke up.

'I'm a bit like Muhammad, except I'm a Christian. I don't drink, I don't want to but my mother sometimes has a glass of wine with her dinner and I don't think there's anything wrong with that. If people do drink, let's look at how it can be used sensibly,' she said.

'Look, everyone's going on about how drink can be OK, but drugs are terrible, tut-tut,' burst out Stephen. 'But isn't that a bit of double-think? I've heard of rich people who can go to their private doctor and get prescriptions for all sorts of things that are perfectly legal, but just as addictive as some illegal drugs. They only take them so that they can feel good. And what about sportsmen, taking all sorts of things just so they can win? Nothing much happens to them! But poor people who want something to help them over a bad patch have to run all sorts of risks to get it!'

'Maybe that's the trouble,' said Michelle thoughtfully. 'People think they can take something to feel good, or not to feel so bad. Could it work if we concentrate on that? Maybe if we . . .'

Information box

Alcoholics Anonymous

Illustration from an Alcoholics Anonymous leaflet

Alcoholics Anonymous is a worldwide fellowship of men and women who help each other to recover from alcoholism. They offer help to anyone who has a drinking problem and wants to do something about it. Since the members are alcoholics themselves, they have a special understanding of each other. Alcoholics Anonymous regard alcohol as an illness. The alcoholic cannot control his or her drinking because they are ill in their body and mind (or emotions). This view is shared by the British Medical Association. Members of Alcoholics Anonymous find support through each other. The groups are open to anyone and they give people the opportunity to talk about their problems and to listen to others who may share the same problem. Even though many people who are in the groups have managed to stop drinking they still come to the meetings of Alcoholics Anonymous not only to help the other members of the group but also to receive encouragement, since it could be easy to give into their addiction when faced with difficulties. Alcoholics Anonymous say that alcoholism is a permanent condition and can never be cured. The only answer is to avoid alcohol altogether. Alcoholics Anonymous give thousands of people the moral strength to stop drinking and start afresh with their lives.

Activities

1. People often talk about being 'addicted' to something they enjoy very much, or something they feel they could not do without, for example a cup of tea in the morning, jogging, certain foods or sweets, a television series, or even work. Brainstorm in class to make a list of as many things as possible that some people may feel addicted to.

   Then discuss whether you think they are 'addictions' and whether you feel there is any harm in them. Here are some questions to help you:

   - How often does the 'addict' have these things, compared with other people?
   - What lengths would the 'addict' go to, to get these things?
   - What happens to the 'addict' if he or she does not get these things?
   - What happens to the 'addict' if he or she goes on having them?

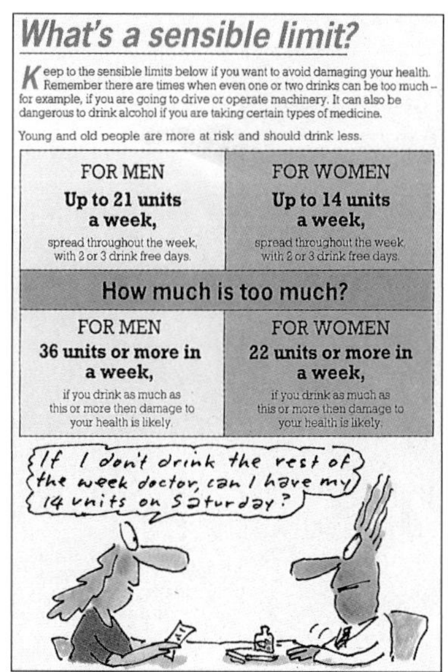

What's a sensible limit?

Keep to the sensible limits below if you want to avoid damaging your health. Remember there are times when even one or two drinks can be too much – for example, if you are going to drive or operate machinery. It can also be dangerous to drink alcohol if you are taking certain types of medicine.

Young and old people are more at risk and should drink less.

FOR MEN	FOR WOMEN
Up to 21 units a week, spread throughout the week, with 2 or 3 drink free days.	**Up to 14 units a week,** spread throughout the week, with 2 or 3 drink free days.
How much is too much?	
FOR MEN	FOR WOMEN
36 units or more in a week, if you drink as much as this or more then damage to your health is likely.	**22 units or more in a week,** if you drink as much as this or more then damage to your health is likely.

2. Conduct a survey on attitudes to alcohol. Think up the questions as a class. Here are some examples:
   - At what age should children be allowed to drink alcohol:
     a) at a party?
     b) at home?
   - Do you agree that most adults drink more than they should?
   - What alcoholic drinks have you tasted?
   - What did you think of them?

   Treat any answers you receive as confidential. Ask some parents to answer the questions as well. Compare the answers.

3. Write and then act out the version of the advertisement Michelle might have thought of.

4. Write the sort of advertisement you would have thought of.

5. What criticisms of your advertisement and Michelle's do you think Mike or Tony might have?

6. Look at existing advertisements or posters on drugs and alcohol. Make a critique of them along the lines of Mike and Tony. Then redesign the advertisements and posters using the same basic ideas that they already contain.

Sources

SIKHISM

Sikhs avoid the use of alcohol, tobacco and drugs, unless they have to be taken for medical reasons. In the Sikh scriptures, several of the Gurus, including Guru Nanak, pointed out the bad effects of these substances:

'Drink not this vicious wine, under any circumstances'. (AG, 553)

'Drinking such a wine, who will earn anything but vice and sin?' (AG, 554)

HINDUISM

The consumption of alcohol or the use of drugs is not forbidden in the Hindu religion, although many Hindus choose to avoid stimulants. This is because drugs and alcohol not only affect the physical state of the human body but they also hamper the spiritual development of the person. Hindus believe that it is necessary to free ourselves from the material things that keep us tied to the cycle of death and rebirth. If a Hindu becomes attached to drugs or alcohol they are forming attachments to this material world and affect his or her karma in this life and in the next rebirth.

CHRISTIANITY

Some Christians are teetotal or abstinent, that is, they do not drink alcohol. They believe that to do so is to encourage others who may have too much to drink and so become alcoholics with all the pain and distress that causes. However, the majority of Christians believe alcohol is a pleasure to be enjoyed in moderation. Jesus himself turned water into wine at the Feast at Cana and used wine at the Last Supper.

Most, if not all, Christians would encourage the proper use of drugs to treat illness, but for no other purpose. Christianity teaches that we are all responsible for our own actions. To dull the mind with alcohol or drugs, or to go into a state where we are no longer responsible for our own actions is to go against our God-given powers of responsibility. This is seen as being both wrong before God and dangerous to others. Many churches run programmes to help alcoholics and drug addicts because they do not condemn people who have become addicts. They want to help them recover so that they can lead full, responsible lives as God wishes them to.

ISLAM

For Muslims, any substance which clouds the mind, impairing its faculties of thought, perception and discernment, is prohibited by Allah. Muslims therefore avoid all intoxicants such as alcohol and intoxicating drugs.

A general principle of Islamic law is that a Muslim should not eat or drink anything which may harm his or her body or health. Muslims are assets to their religion and to the Muslim community, and their lives, health, wealth and all that Allah has given them are a trust which they are not permitted to squander.

NORTH AMERICAN INDIANS

The peyote plant will cause hallucinations, if taken in sufficient quantities. It was, and still is, used in religious practices by North American Indians and is considered a sacrament in their religion.

The Indians either chew an appropriate quantity of the plant or brew a tea from it. This is usually taken at an all-night, dignified ceremony, usually within a teepee with a priest or 'road chief' in charge who directs the ceremony. After taking the plant, worshippers see visions and participate in experiences which draw them all together towards their communities' teachings.

In the nineteenth century, bands of these Indians grouped together to form the North American Church so that they would have both legal and religious protection from outsiders who criticised their practices. Members of the Church see themselves as basically practising Christian principles and lifestyle. They emphasise the idea of brotherly love, self-reliance, hard work, and avoidance of alcohol.

Not all Indians or all Indian tribes approve of the hallucinations that the peyote or any other plant can cause. The taking of the peyote does, however, have a long and respected tradition and the effects of it are not seen as strange or threatening but may even be welcomed and highly valued. It is also important to remember that we hear little of addiction to drugs (other than alcohol) among American Indians.

JUDAISM

Wine has always been a feature of Jewish religion. Wine is drunk as part of the Sabbath celebration which lasts from sunset on Friday evening to sunset on Saturday evening. There is an obligation to drink four glasses of wine on Passover Day although the wine drunk is not very potent. Wine is also drunk at festivals of celebration such as Purim.

The excessive use of alcohol and the taking of drugs (except under medical supervision) are condemned because they prevent a human being from exercising their God given gifts of the mind and intelligence. It is considered a destruction of life and Jews consider life to be the most sacred of all things.

Role-play

1. There are many different groups interested in the promotion and sale of alcohol. There are the brewers, the advertising people, the pubs and wine shops, the police and many religious people. They all view drinking from different angles. As a class, plan a TV documentary on drinking. Divide the class into different interest groups, such as the ones listed above. You might be able to think of other groups who would have an interest.

   Each group should work out a basic position statement lasting no more than one minute. These should be presented with perhaps one person as the TV anchorperson who acts as an intermediary between the groups.

   After each group has presented its case, the anchorperson should try to encourage an argument between the different groups, based upon what they have said.

   After this session, each group should then be given another chance to write another one minute presentation in which they answer the major criticisms of what they said in the first session.

2. Drugs are an essential part of medical care. They can ease pain and help at times of distress. But they can also destroy people's lives if they are used in the wrong way.

   It is also difficult to know how to stop people taking drugs. The story about the advertisement shows that.

   Try to work out the following situation. A local supermarket sells all the usual things such places offer: food, alcohol, do-it-yourself equipment, including glues and so on. However, the area has a bad history of drunks, violence arising from alcohol, glue sniffers and other types of solvent abuse. A group of parents and other citizens have written to the manager of the supermarket complaining that the supermarket does nothing to stop such abuse. They are not suggesting that the shop stops selling things but that they take steps to warn people about alcohol and solvent abuse.

   In this case, start by being the citizens group and write the letter to the supermarket manager. You can make it as strong as you like, but be polite! Also, in the group are some who for different reasons feel that there should be no alcohol on sale in the store. How would the group arrive at an agreed text for the letter and what would it say?

   Then switch roles. Now you are the managers and staff of the shop. You have to respond to this letter! In the group are the manager and his top staff, plus representatives from the staff union. One of these is a manager of the wine shop in the store. She has a son who has had drink problems and this would affect what she thinks.

   First of all, what is the overall response of the group to the letter? Secondly, what practical steps to try to prevent abuse can the store take? Thirdly, what suggestions do you have for the wider community to help the store deal with people who misuse alcohol and solvents? Put all this together into a package which you offer to the community.

The Competition

Alison, Pallavi and Karen had one thing in common. All three were very keen on entering competitions. Not that they were very good. So far, Alison had won a stuffed toy, Pallavi, a weekend for two in Skegness and Karen, a pen set. But this did not stop them. Any competition was fair game.

'I've found a new competition,' said Pallavi one morning. 'It looks very easy. All we've got to do is write a romantic short story about a first boyfriend and we could win a holiday in Italy, or a treasure trove worth £500.'

The other two gathered round to study the competition details in the magazine. 'No problem,' said Karen. 'Shall we meet at lunchtime?' They all agreed.

At first, it did seem easy. 'So what are we going to call them?' asked Alison. 'How about Steve and Julie?' said Karen. Then they started to write. The first attempt soon ran into difficulties.

'Julie and Steve had been in the same group for about a year before they noticed each other. Then one day, Steve realised how much he liked Julie,' wrote Pallavi.

'Their eyes met across the crowded restaurant. The diamonds in Julie's necklace sparkled – just like her. "I've got to meet this wonderful woman," said Steve and he ordered another bottle of champagne,' wrote Alison.

'Their bodies moved to the rhythm of the music as the band got into their routine. "Hi, I'm Steve," said Steve. "Like to dance with me?" he asked,' wrote Karen.

'Oh come on,' said Karen, 'what's with all the

diamonds and champagne? That's just not real.' 'Well I don't think Pallavi's is real,' replied Alison. 'No one waits that long.'

'Rubbish,' said Karen, 'it's not all "love at first sight." You often find you like someone when they've been around a while. Like Andy and Sharon at church. They've been in the youth club for ages together, but have only just started going out.'

So, by a process of choice they decided to use Pallavi's opening. They then agreed on what happened next. Julie invites Steve to the pictures. 'There, that's striking a blow for women's rights,' laughed Alison.

'That might win us the prize, but I daren't show my Mum that,' said Pallavi. 'It's not done in my family for women to start something – at least, not officially,' she said with a wink. It was what should happen after that that they disagreed about.

'Seated in the park, as the evening drew to an end, Steve kissed Julie. It was like a dream come true,' wrote Alison.

'As Steve took Julie home he held her hand. Neither of them knew quite what to say or do. At her door, Steve asked if he could kiss her,' wrote Pallavi.

'It was as if a tide of passion was released. Steve held Julie to him and she sighed as she sank into his arms,' wrote Karen. When the others criticised her, Karen said, 'Well at least it's got some excitement in it. Yours are too soft.'

'That may be,' said Alison, 'but ours are a lot more likely. All that rubbish about falling into people's arms. It just doesn't happen.'

'I'm not sure we can do this,' said Pallavi. 'I mean, it's not easy is it? I suppose we could just write romantic stuff, but it's not really real. My parents are quite liberal, but if I write about how boys who like me have to behave, the readers would be bored in a few minutes.'

'No. You're right,' said Alison. 'I think most people find each other slowly. You know, over time. The problem with us is we are trying to pack everything into not just a short story but a short period of time.'

The discussion went on for some time. Eventually they moved on from the first kiss to the first row. It was agreed that the row would most likely be about another person (this was Pallavi's suggestion), or about sex (this was Alison's suggestion) or about money (Karen's idea).

Activities

1. Continue the story by writing about the three different reasons for the row between Julie and Steve. Try to think through the different personalities and backgrounds of Alison, Karen and Pallavi and decide what they believe.
2. Try to write a romantic short story yourself or in a group. Have two versions:
   - an 'over-the-top' version
   - a realistic version.
3. Write out and then act either the continuing debate between Alison, Pallavi and Karen, or the short stories. Ask others in the class to comment on how realistic your versions are.
4. What are the characteristics you would look for in a girlfriend or boyfriend?
5. What are the things that are most likely to cause arguments with your boyfriend or girlfriend and with your parents?

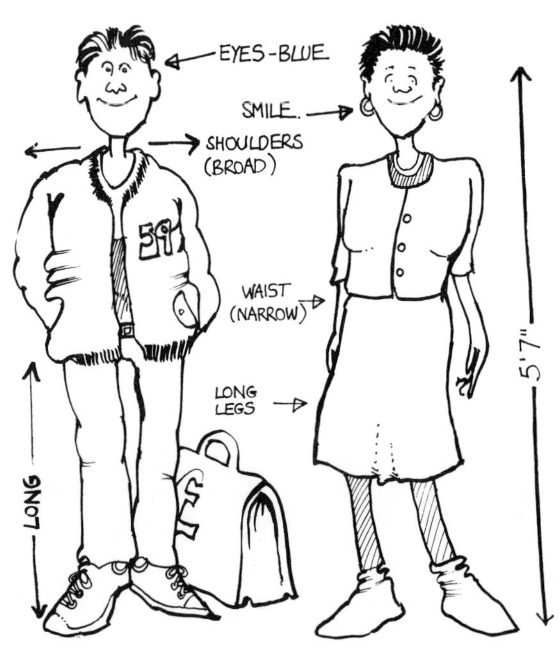

The Parting

Nemu and Josh Solanki had been married for over 40 years. They had become engaged when they were both very young. Their families lived in the same town in North India and had always got on well. It seemed only natural that they should be linked by a marriage. Nemu was a strong young man of 16 when he and Josh, who was nearly 16, got married. They had only met once to discuss the marriage, but that was normal. Their parents arranged it all and both Nemu and Josh trusted their parents' choice of a marriage partner.

Life had been quite good to the Solankis. When their eldest child was two, they had moved to the United Kingdom. Here, Mr Solanki had worked very hard and the family had a comfortable lifestyle. Their children had all gone through school and had done very well for themselves. Now the youngest one was getting married and that meant they were all established with their own homes and families.

But this youngest daughter had not been easy. She had been born and raised in England. She did not really think like a traditional Hindu should. She wanted to have her own boyfriends and to go out with whomever she wanted. Her father, Nemu, had to put his foot down. There had been a great row. The daughter, whose name was Rana, but who was called Ana by her English friends, had stormed out of the house. She had threatened to go to live with her current boyfriend, Mark, but her brothers and sisters persuaded her not to. It would have meant the end of her being a member of the family as far as her parents were concerned.

Finally, a compromise had been reached. Rana did choose her own husband, but only after the family had met him and approved of him. There were some in the community who muttered about falling standards, but Nemu and Josh were realists. They wanted Rana to be happy, but they also knew that for a marriage to last, it usually needs the support of both families.

So now that was all behind them. They had grandchildren of whom they were very fond, but life seemed a little pointless and without meaning. Nemu and Josh discussed their feelings and came to a decision.

When they told the family what they planned to do, the family were very shocked.

'What! But why? Don't you like each other or us any longer?' said one.

'What will you live on?' asked another.

For Nemu and Josh had decided that Nemu would take sanyasin. This meant that he would leave the family and travel back to India. There he would become a wandering holy man, teaching about the Hindu philosophy of life and showing people that work, money and family were not the most important things in life. Josh meanwhile would also leave the family and would travel to one of the holy cities. There she would go to live with other widows for it would be as if Nemu had died. He would no longer be her husband nor she his wife. In the holy place, Josh would serve the gods at the shrines and live out her life until she died.

The family was very upset. They felt rejected by their parents. But gradually they became used to the idea. As Nemu said, 'We have enjoyed being married for over 40 years. We love you all so much, but one day we will both die anyway and leave you behind. We have left you all with money and lives which you can live without us. Now we want to give ourselves to the wider family of the world. Please don't be selfish with us. We will always love you, but there are many out there who need our care and need to be reminded that money and family are not everything.'

The family accepted that if this was really what their parents wanted, they would not stop them. Apparently, in old India it used to be quite common. In the UK it is very rare. It made many other families in the Hindu community look again at what they did and what they believed and led some to change certain ways they behaved to be a better example of Hindu beliefs. And, on the appointed day, Nemu and Josh took a long and touching farewell from their family and from each other, and set off, in different directions, to start the last and newest phase of their lives.

Information box

Sanyasin

Bathing in the sacred river Ganges

Hindus believe that we are tied to a cycle of death and rebirth and, although it is possible to escape from this cycle, our thoughtless actions keep us tied here. Everything we do has an effect on something or someone, and as we go through life we build up a store of good and bad deeds called karma. Hindus believe that our karma determines whether we are reborn to a difficult or easy life, whether we are healthy or disabled, even whether we are born as a human, animal or a plant. It is, however, possible to escape rebirth if we let go of the material things that keep us tied to this life. By doing this it is possible to become one with the Supreme Being who is in all life. This is why men and women renounce their worldly possessions to become sanyasin. It is a way to understand the nature of the Supreme Being and hopefully break the ties of rebirth.

Activities

1. Why do you think Nemu and Josh's parents arranged their marriage? Why do you think Nemu and Josh agreed to the marriage and do you think their marriage has been a success?

2. You could summarise the course of Nemu and Josh's marriage like this:
   Parents arranged marriage
   Married at age 16
   Gradually came to love each other
   Children born
   Children grow up
   Children married
   Grandchildren born
   Separate to concentrate on religion.

   Think of two different marriages, either of people you know, or imaginary, and summarise the main stages in the marriage in the same way. Perhaps make one marriage happy and the other unhappy.

3. Write two letters that you think Nemu and Josh's children might send to their parents. Their daughter is happy for her parents and is writing to tell them what she feels about them taking sanyasin. Their son is still troubled that they have chosen sanyasin and is writing to tell them about his worries.

The Date

'I could make him notice me if I wanted to!'

'Oh, sure,' laughed Judy's friends, 'if you wanted to! Go on, then, show us how!'

Judy put a hand behind her head and swung her hips a little. But it was not really convincing, even to her. Everyone else just groaned. 'All right, maybe it's not that simple. But I still think it could be done. And I think someone ought to do it. Who does he think he is, going round with his nose in the air, as if girls just didn't exist! It's time someone taught him that you can't just ignore half the human race.'

'I reckon you'd stand a better chance if you rolled yourself in mud and dressed up as a football!' joked Sally. 'The thing is with Ian, if it's not on the football pitch, he doesn't see it. His whole life revolves around sport.'

'Well, it shouldn't. It would do him good to have another interest in life,' said Judy.

'Oh, come on, Judy,' said Christine, 'you're not interested in what would do Ian good. And you're not interested in that feminist line about ignoring half the human race. You're just annoyed because he doesn't notice you!'

'That's not it, and I'll prove it to you!' cried Judy. 'Look, I'll bet you five pounds I can get him to ask me out. And then when he does, I'll turn him down flat. That'll teach him and you what I think of him!'

The others laughed, feeling a little uncomfortable, and let the subject drop. Judy would not carry out her threat – she had only said it in the heat of the moment, and Ian was OK really. All right, he was sports mad, and his friends were all boys, but nobody really thought he looked down on girls. Judy would soon give up when she got no reaction.

But she did get a reaction. No one was quite sure how it happened, but as the weeks went by, Ian did seem to be taking more notice of Judy. Nothing much – sometimes a grin and a wave as he came off the football pitch, sometimes checking his homework with her – 'What did you put for question 3?' And certainly Judy made sure that she was always around when Ian was doing anything interesting.

Then one day Sally came up to the others in great excitement just as they were leaving school.

'Come and watch!' she said. 'I reckon Judy's going to win her bet after all! You know she's in that drama rehearsal, and it's gone on a bit late? Well, I've just seen Ian hanging around outside the hall. He's trying to look as if he's not doing anything much there, and a couple of times he's got up and begun to leave, then he sort of hesitated and turned back. You can see him from the top of the stairs. Come on!' and she ran back to her observation post.

One or two of the girls had not heard of the bet that Judy had made. When Caroline heard about it, she was indignant. 'That's horrible! How could she do it?'

Leila simply said 'I could never, ever do that in a million years!' and walked away down the corridor. No one could work out whether the note in her voice was envy or disgust.

'Oh, come on!' said Christine, 'Haven't you heard of the battle of the sexes? That's what adult life is all about, and if you don't fight for your side you'll get beaten. Judy didn't mean anything serious by it.'

'That's exactly what I mean – she's made a game of it. Maybe Ian does think he's the next England football star, but that's better than making a game out of other people.'

The argument went on so long that in the end it was only Sally who saw Ian approach Judy as she came out of the hall. It was only Sally who saw Judy hesitate briefly, then say a few words and walk away. And it was only Sally who saw the look on Ian's face as he ran out of the school.

But when Sally cornered Judy the next day to congratulate her on winning her bet, Judy did not seem all that interested.

'What did you say to him, Judy? You certainly taught him what's what! He hasn't even turned up in school today!'

'Hasn't he?' said Judy, 'I didn't know that. But it's nothing to do with me.'

Activities

1. Leila is a Muslim. Why do you think she said what she said?
2. Why do you think that Ian did not come to school? Is Judy right in saying 'It's nothing to do with me'?
3. If Ian's friends knew what had happened, what do you think they would say to him? What would you say?
4. If Judy's mother knew what had happened, what do you think she would say to Judy? What would you say?

Sources

HINDUISM

Krishna says the sexual act is sacred. Sex is, therefore, seen as a sacred thing.

In Hindu culture, the higher someone's social position, the more strictly they have to follow rules governing sexual behaviour. The brahmin (priest or teacher) is expected to be very self-controlled within marriage. Prayers have to be said before sex and it is performed in a religious way. The child that is born out of this union is a very good child, while the child that is born out of lust will be influenced by lust during his or her life.

Hindu scriptures teach that the sexual attraction between men and women is what keeps us in the cycle of birth and death. Men are attracted to the form of women and as a result are born female in their next birth and women are attracted to the form of men and so they are born male in their next birth.

Those who are following a spiritual life will practise celibacy, then marry and have sex in a religious way to produce children. On entering middle age the husband and wife would then become celibate again. In old age they may then take the vows of complete celibacy.

There is also the idea of sanyas in Hinduism, when a man or woman leaves their partner and renounces all material things to become a sanyasin: he or she concentrates completely on their spritual life to escape the cycles of death and rebirth.

SIKHISM

Self-control and self-discipline are regarded as important virtues throughout life for a Sikh and these apply equally to sexual activity. Marriage is accepted as a normal condition of life. Every Sikh is expected to lead a married life and sex outside marriage is prohibited in the Sikh Code of Discipline called 'Rahat-maryada'.

Whilst it is usual for adolescent boys and girls to mix together in Western societies, this goes against the Sikh tradition as it is believed that this can lead to illicit love. However, in Sikh families there is usually no objection to a Sikh boy meeting a girl of about his age when it is out of a desire to be married.

Marriage in Sikh religion is 'arranged' or 'assisted'. According to the Sikh tradition, the unit is the family and not the individual, and as such it is the duty of the head of the family to arrange the marriages. The parents consult their children before carrying out any marriage arrangements and it is only when the boy or girl shows some interest that the parents will proceed further with the matter.

Sikhism forbids a marriage forced either on the girl or the boy and both give their consent to the priest or granthi before he proceeds with the marriage ceremony.

In the Sikh faith homosexuality is forbidden and is regarded as unnatural and immoral.

In the Sikh holy book, the Adi Granth, it says:

> 'Having sex with another woman is as dangerous as the sting of a poisonous snake'. (AG, 403)
>
> 'Pollution of the eyes is caused by coveting another's wife or wealth'. (AG, 472)

JUDAISM

Jews believe in sex within marriage and that children from this union are a great blessing. The Jewish teachings are opposed in principle to any form of homosexuality or unnatural practice. There is no tradition of celibacy or monasticism within the Jewish faith and there are no Jewish monks or nuns.

CHRISTIANITY

Christianity teaches that the normal state for men and women is marriage. In some churches, notably the Roman Catholic Church, divorce is forbidden. Most churches forbid sex before marriage and practising homosexuality. However, increasingly, priests and other Christians have stressed that what is important in a relationship, in or out of marriage, is love, compassion and a true concern for the other person. This belief that a relationship has to be for the benefit of both partners means many churches now allow divorce, though they stress that people should try all they can to keep a marriage together. It also means that many clergy will marry people who have lived together before coming to be married.

In some churches, homosexuals are supported as long as they are in a loving long-term relationship - even though the same churches still teach that a truly proper relationship should be between a man and a woman. No church approves of casual sex or of exploitation of men's or women's bodies for use in pornography or any other way which uses them unlovingly or in an exploitative manner.

The Church, in certain cases, also respects celibacy. In the Orthodox, Roman Catholic and certain types of Anglican Churches, it is accepted that a man or woman can give up the idea of marriage in order to live, without sex, in a religious community, wedded to the service of Christ.

> Human sexuality is one of God's good gifts. Like other of God's gifts, such as music or athletic ability, it consists of both biological and spiritual elements. As with other of God's gifts, what matters is how the gift is used. A gift can be used selfishly or for others; it can be exploited or developed; it can be used for promoting relationships or destroying them. In short, human sexuality can be for God's glory or it can be a denial of God's hope for us.
>
> (*Report of the Commission on Human Sexuality to the Methodist Conference 1990*)

ISLAM

Because Islam stresses chastity and modesty so strongly, there is little contact between young men and young women in most parts of the Muslim world. Except among the most Westernised, boys and girls do not mix or go out with each other. Love is considered very important in Muslim marriage, but for Muslim couples love grows between them after they are married rather than before. Marriages are therefore usually arranged by the parents, although the young people can express a preference and say what they want in a marriage partner.

In Islam marriage is not a religious sacrament, but a legal, binding contract between the man and the woman. But the relationship between husband and wife is described and supported in the Qur'an in vivid language:

> 'They (wives) are your garments and you are their garments.' (Chapter 2, v. 187)

This means that each person is the protection, covering, support and adornment of the other. They should each fulfil the other's sexual needs, and keep themselves for each other, as well as caring for each other's needs in other ways.

If disagreements arise between the couple, every attempt is made to resolve them, and the families of the couple play an important part in supporting and fostering their relationship. But if this proves impossible, Islam allows divorce as a last resort.

Role-play

1. Relationships, or the need for relationships, are often used for advertising purposes. The usual sales pitch is that if you eat, wear, smoke or drink this particular product, then men and women will rush to be your friend!

   The situation you have to work on concerns an old firm of chocolate manufacturers. Having been set up in the eighteenth century to provide a food which the poor could also afford and an alternative drink to alcohol, the firm has a long history of moral concern. This is watched over by an Ethics Committee who decide what is right and wrong in their business dealings. The firm invites well-known religious figures from all the main faiths as well as others, to advise them on their work. The group has very high standards.

   Recently a new managing director and team of experts have been appointed to give the firm a more go-ahead, profitable profile. They have decided to update some of the firm's products and make them more appealing. The first one they choose is the *Dolphin Bar* – a popular chocolate bar. To do this they hire a famous and very successful advertising agency.

Part 1

An advertising agency has been asked to design an advertisement that gives a new image to the chocolate bar. They decide to indicate that eating this bar makes you more attractive to others. They also change the name of the bar to make it more enticing and romantic.

As a class or in groups decide what the new advertisement will say, what kind of images it will use and what kind of music or commentary will accompany the advertisement.

Part 2

The class splits into three groups. The first group is the Ethics Committee. They know that there are big changes about to happen, but are not sure quite what they are, except that the words 'sex' and 'romance' have been mentioned. They have to decide what they think about these changes, and if they should oppose them. But they must also come up with an alternative way to promote the bar without exploitation of sexual imagery.

The manager and his team make up the second group. They want to push the new image, but they also know that they cannot overrule the Ethics Committee. How would they approach this problem? They have to produce arguments to say why this new image is acceptable. If changes have to be made, they need to be acceptable to the other groups and also make the product sell.

Finally, there is the advertising agency. They think they have the answer and feel they can justify using sexual imagery and the idea that if you eat this bar your romantic life will improve.

Each group in class prepares its case. Then listen to each of the other groups and finally vote as if you were a jury deciding which group should have its way.

2. You have decided to set up a marriage bureau. You want it to be romantic and for people to find a partner who will make them happy for life. You have to decide what the basic questionnaire should ask. You need to find out information about people and what kind of partner and relationship they are looking for. You also know that some people use such agencies to find victims for crime or exploitation.

So how do you set out a questionnaire which will discover the real intentions and interests of people, and will help you match people with a good partner?

You also have to give guidelines for people who want to make a video which can be sent to interested partners. Again, you have to remember that people can make themselves look very foolish when making ordinary videos, let alone ones which they hope will win them a husband or wife!

Split into pairs for this. Then let each pair read out their results and see what the rest of the class make of it!

A Wealth of Tales

The faiths of the world are rich in stories which tell us more than any lecture or book could ever do. The following are just a few stories on the theme of money and wealth.

There was once a rich man who asked his friends, 'What use will all my hard work and piles of money be on the day of my death?' His friends suggested that if this worried him, he should give his money to the poor and to charities. This way he would be able to approach the day of his death happy in the knowledge that he would be accepted in Heaven.

The rich man thought this a good idea, but swore that he would only give to a person who was so poor and in such great need that he had given up hope in life.

One day, walking near the city, the rich man saw what he thought was just such a person. The poor man was dressed in filthy rags and sitting alone. The rich man decided that here was a man who had abandoned all hope in life and so gave him a vast sum of money.

The poor man was astonished. 'Why have you given me so much money?' he asked. 'Because I swore I would only give to someone who has lost all hope in life,' replied the rich man.

'Then take back your money,' said the poor man angrily. 'I may be poor but I believe in God and in His Grace. He could restore me to health and wealth if He wished. While I believe this I have not given up hope. So don't insult me!'

The rich man was very taken aback. 'Is this how you respond to my generosity? Have I really done you such an insult for you to be so rude to me?'

'You, sir,' said the poor man, 'are under the impression that you have done me a favour. It is just the opposite. It is as if you have killed me with your so-called 'compassion'. For only a dead man has given up hope in life.'

The rabbi of a town visited the wealthiest man in the community. The rabbi was collecting money for the orphanage. The rich man told him he would give nothing!

'If you will give some money, I will sell you my share in Paradise,' said the rabbi. The rich man was delighted with this offer, for there was no other way he would get into Paradise! So he gave the rabbi enough money to help to rebuild the orphanage.

The rabbi's followers were very upset when they heard what he had done. 'Rabbi, how could you have possibly done such a thing?' they asked. The rabbi replied, 'Twice a day I say my prayers. I say "Love thy God with all thy heart, with all thy soul and with all thy possessions". My sons, I am only a poor rabbi. What are my possessions? All that I possess is my share in Paradise, and to serve God's children, His orphans, I am ready to give up even that.'

A rich man was asked once by his priest, 'Do you give much to charity?' The rich man replied, 'God be praised, I give enough. But I am a modest man, father – I don't say much about it.'

The priest replied, 'Say more about it – and give more!'

The Christian Desert Fathers lived in the third century CE. They felt that the world and the Church had become too concerned with money and possessions, so they lived as monks in the North African desert with as few possessions as possible, and spent their time in prayer. One day a wealthy man from the town visited one of the priests in the desert, and gave him a basket of gold pieces.

'Share this out amongst your brother monks,' he said. But the priest refused to accept the gift.

'They have no need of it,' he said.

The wealthy man would not take back his gold.

'Put it at the door of the church,' he said, 'and tell all the monks that if anyone has any need, he should take it.'

So the basket stood outside the church, and for several days the wealthy man watched as the monks went in and out on their way to prayers. Not one of them touched it, or even cared enough to look at it. After a few days the wealthy man took his gold back to town and thought long and hard about what had happened.

There was once a Buddhist householder who had a gift for making money. Whatever he did not need he changed into gold and then placed it in a golden urn. He was afraid to let the urn out of his sight and even slept with it by his pillow. Eventually he had saved enough money that he had seven urns full of gold; fearing that someone might try to take them from him, he hid them deep down in the ground in his garden. As he grew older he filled even more urns with gold and continued to hide them but, finally, he fell ill and died.

Because he was so attached to the gold during his life he was reborn as a poisonous snake who jealously guarded the golden urns. During his life as a snake he thought of his previous life and how he had turned his back on everyone for the love of his money. He reflected on his current life as a snake, forever bound to lie in the ground coiled around the urns. He grew unhappy and restless and finally he found a way to free himself from this suffering. One day he beckoned a passer-by into the grounds and begged him to take the gold and give it to charity. The passer-by did as he was asked and the snake was eventually freed from his suffering.

There was once a poor tailor who lived by himself. He did not have much money, but he made enough to live on by making and selling clothes. One day a stranger gave him an old leather purse and told him it was magic.

'Every time you open it you will find a gold coin inside. Take out the coin, and next time you open it there will be another one. There is only one condition. You must not spend any of the money until you have thrown the purse in the river. If you do, you will die!'

And so saying, the mysterious stranger disappeared.

Full of curiosity the tailor looked inside the purse. Sure enough, there was a gold coin. Eagerly, the tailor snatched it out and put it in his pocket.

When he opened the purse again, there was another gold coin. Then the tailor thought about

the stranger's warning, 'You cannot spend the money until the purse has been thrown in the river.'

He needed to buy food for his supper but he didn't want to throw away the purse and so he hungrily ran home and shut the door of his house firmly behind him. He spent a happy hour taking coin after coin out of the purse and storing them under the floorboards. At the end of the hour he had a good store, and he was tired and hungry. He looked at the money. 'It's certainly enough to let me live comfortably but if I fell ill, or had trouble with my business, it wouldn't last me long. I need more money.'

So he spent another hour taking coins out of the purse and storing them away. By this time his stomach was rumbling alarmingly as he looked at his store of coins.

'Well, it's enough to let me live quite comfortably no matter what happens to my business. Perhaps I should stop and get my supper. But on the other hand, if I take out some more money, I could live in greater luxury.'

And as the tailor sat thinking of the wonderful life he could lead with his newly found wealth he continued to take coins out of the purse.

It was several days before the tailor's friends noticed that he had not been seen, and his shop had not opened. For several days more they wondered what to do about it. They knocked on his door, but got no answer. Eventually they broke his door down and went in. There on the floor lay the tailor, dead of starvation. And there beside him lay a huge pile of gold coins, and an old brown purse.

'We don't understand it,' said his friends, 'How could he starve when he had so much money, and the shops are full of food?'

Activities

1. Why had the tailor starved to death?
2. Imagine you had just won three million pounds. You decide to keep a reasonable amount for yourself, and give the rest away to charity. Make a list of the things that you would definitely want to buy before you gave your money away, and write down the approximate cost of them. Write down how much you would want to keep 'for a rainy day'.

   How much is left to give away?
3. There are many popular songs about money, for example 'If I were a rich man', 'Can't buy me love'. It is quite likely that there is one in the pop charts at the moment. Brainstorm as a class to think of as many songs about money as you can. Write down the words of some of them. What attitude to money does each one represent?
4. All these stories have a moral: some of them are funny, some of them are surprising or seem contradictory. Write your own story about money in a similar style. Make sure it has a moral, but perhaps not an obvious one.

Success

To Colin, his brother Philip was everything he wanted to be. Ten years older than him, Philip was successful with a big S. Everything had always worked out easy for Philip. He had been good at almost everything. He had always had girlfriends and was very popular at school. He and Dana had been going out since they were both 18 and had been married now for three years.

By the time he was 19, Philip had a good salary working as a trainee salesman for a big chemical company. By the time he was 20, he owned a BMW car and had taken out a mortgage on the big house where he and Dana now lived. For the past four years Philip had been top salesman of the year and for most months he was top salesman of the month.

At first Dana had enjoyed Philip's success. 'The money's great,' she told his mum when she admired her new hairstyle and clothes. 'The only trouble is, Philip's not here to appreciate it. I see less of him now than when we were going out together! I'm not really complaining, but I do feel left out of his life. I don't matter any more.'

So, in order not to be left out, Dana had started her own business, from the house. She ran a very expensive, but good catering service. Clients would ask her to prepare meals for special occasions. She was so successful that she now had four assistants and was earning very good money.

But this did not improve their relationship. Philip and Dana hardly saw each other and when they did, they were usually tired. To the outside world however, and to Colin, they were the perfect example of a successful couple. When the final blow came, Colin could not believe it. And all over a newspaper article, so he thought.

The magazine *Good Cooking* wanted to do a feature on Dana and her cooking. She was delighted but Philip was not. Especially when he read the first draft of the article and found he was mentioned simply as 'her husband, a salesman'.

'I'm director of the sales team. This just makes me sound cheap,' he complained. 'And why are you getting all this attention?' he continued angrily. 'I'm the successful one around here. You wouldn't be able to do your little cooking parties if I didn't pay the bills for the house and everything.'

'Oh, yes, my business is 'parties', but when you're out five nights a week drinking and dining with customers, that's 'work', isn't it! You don't value me enough to come home before bedtime, so I've found something else where I am valued. And now you want to take that away from me, just because you're jealous!'

'How dare you! I've worked like a slave these last few years, to build a comfortable life for you, a bit of security. You were quite happy to sit back and spend the money I earned, and now you're throwing all that in my face!'

Two days later Dana left their home. Colin asked his mother what had happened. 'Well, she says she loves Philip still, but that he's changed. Trouble is though, they've both changed. They don't seem to actually need each other now. Too busy being successful.'

Philip carried on as though nothing had happened for a while. He refused to talk about Dana and simply buried himself in his work. He worked ridiculously long hours but instead of it making him even more successful, he began to slip back. His sales figures dropped and he began to get very awkward to work with. The company began to wonder if he was doing his job properly.

Dana continued her successful business from a small shop she rented. But Colin's mum thought that she was not happy.

Five months later Philip tried to kill himself. His sales figures were the worst of the entire company and he was given a lower position and a lower salary. He did not have the company car any more and he felt his whole world was crashing in around him. None of the family knew anything

about it until the hospital called. Then Dana rushed to his bedside and sat with him the whole time.

Colin hoped this would mean a happy ending. But it was not as simple as that. Philip lost his job and sat in hospital moping about it. 'It's all right, Philip,' said Dana. 'I'll move back in – I never wanted to leave you, you know. I can earn enough for both of us while you look for something else – something with less pressure,'

'And how do you think that would make me feel?' muttered Philip.

'Well, I suppose, much the same as I felt when you were out working all the time and I felt utterly useless. It's hard, but for a few months it might be good for you.'

That hurt, and the two of them only just stopped short of another quarrel. They wanted to make a success of their relationship – a different sort of success this time – but they had a long way to go.

Activities

1. Why did Philip try to commit suicide? Was it because his work was not going well or for some other reason?

2. Do you think that Philip and Dana will eventually make 'a different sort of success' out of their lives? Write an account of their lives a year after this story ends.

3. If you hear someone described as 'successful', what does this mean to you? Draw a picture of or write a song about a successful person.

4. What do you spend your money on? How much do you save?

5. How much money would you expect to earn when you are 25? What sort of job would you want?

6. There are many proverbs about money. Some are given below. Brainstorm in class to think of others. Take one or two and discuss exactly what they mean. In groups, take one of the proverbs and make a short play that illustrates it.

   'The best things in life are free.'
   'All that glitters is not gold.'
   'The love of money is the root of all evil.'
   (This is a quotation from the Bible, (1 Timothy 6:10), and is often misquoted as 'money is the root of all evil.')

Sources

JUDAISM

Wealth has traditionally been seen as a reward from God for a virtuous and hard working life. In the Jewish religion there is an obligation to give to charity which has always been, and still is, taken very seriously. Ten per cent of one's income was generally given and even those who were poor themselves were expected to give something as it was believed that even the poorest beggar could find someone worse off than himself. The second priority for Jews was to provide education for their sons, and in the past, also to provide dowries to ensure good marriages for their daughters.

Acquiring knowledge has always been regarded more highly than acquiring wealth. Traditionally the most important job was that of the rabbi. Today his position has been usurped by the professionals, and the most admired now are the doctors, lawyers and scientists. Jewish society believes that poverty is not a good thing and it is the requirement of all Jews to help improve the lives of the poor.

ISLAM

As one of the Five Pillars of the Muslim faith, every Muslim family who can afford it has to give some of their money to the poor and the needy. This amount is worked out according to strict rules and usually equal to one fortieth of everything they own, not counting their home, furniture, car, or other essential possessions.

This money, called zakat, is seen as an obligation or duty. By taking money from the rich and giving it to the poor and to where it is really needed, zakat helps to create equality in Muslim society.

> 'He is not a true Muslim who eats his fill when his next door neighbour is hungry'. (Prophet Bukhari)

The ultimate aim of zakat is to eliminate poverty. It is said that the system worked so well in the early days that Umar, the second Caliph, who led the Muslims after the death of Muhammad, could not find any poor people to give zakat to in all Arabia.

Islam disagrees strongly with the practice of charging interest on money and a Muslim is strictly forbidden from either charging or paying interest. Muslims believe that no one should make money simply by lending money. If someone has more money than they need, they should do something practical with it that would benefit society. If they want to earn more money, they should work for it like everybody else.

BUDDHISM

Buddhists believe that our present wealth is a reflection of our actions in the past and the way in which we make and handle money now will affect our circumstances in the future. Good actions lead to good effects, bad actions to bad effects and neutral actions to neutral effects. This is known as the chain of cause and effect but it is very difficult for ordinary human beings to see how it works.

Buddhists believe that we should not put our energies into developing material wealth but should concentrate on developing the qualities of kindness, love and compassion.

Performing acts of generosity is an important part of the Buddha's teachings. Good deeds build up a store of merit which have positive effects in this life and in the next. There are two types of generosity that bring merit: one is for the poor and the sick, that is for people of this world; and the other is for higher beings where generosity is expressed through offerings to the shrine and to monks. The most important part of being wealthy is being able to help others with that money.

Buddhists believe that poverty is a major cause of corruption in society. Poverty may drive people to theft, lying and violence but, if compassion and generosity can be shown to the poor, these evils may be avoided. Buddhists also believe that those who are wealthy and refuse to part with their money will eventually be poor themselves.

CHRISTIANITY

Jesus taught that no one can have two masters. Either you serve God or you serve mammon (Matthew 6:24). This teaching has meant that over the centuries, many Christians have seen mammon – the powers of this world, but especially the pursuit of wealth and power – as being unacceptable to true Christians. Jesus also taught that you should pay what was owed to the government and do what was right before God (Mark 12:17). This meant that Christians were never against money itself, but against it taking over people's lives.

For many hundreds, even over a thousand years, Christians were forbidden by the Church to practise usury. The making of money out of lending money was condemned. However, as modern capitalism began to develop, this teaching was abandoned and many of the Protestant churches never taught it at all.

Today, all the main Christian denominations teach that money has to be used for the good of all. They all teach that unequal distribution

Christianity continued

of wealth means injustice and that this is against the will of God. They try to help Christians who live in the complex world of present day economics to use their money wisely – such as through ethical investment funds – and by encouraging the giving of money and time to charities, the church and other causes. St Paul put it very neatly – 'The love of money is the root of all evil' (1 Timothy 6:10). The Church tries to prevent Christians worshipping money, and tries to persuade them to use money for the love of God.

Role-play

1. As students, you are a big market which advertisers, companies and banks try to get hold of. You have money to spend, maybe not as much as you like, but some. The most important thing about you is that companies know that if you start buying their goods now, then you will probably continue to buy for years to come. So you are a target group and millions of pounds is spent trying to capture your money!

   It is a tough world out there and the companies will go to almost any lengths to get your attention and, of course, your money. So, you have to learn to survive and to find out how to make up your own mind and not be tricked or persuaded into what you buy.

   It is a bit like a battle, so we want you to plan a counter-offensive. Imagine that you have met someone who has become your friend, but has never lived in our kind of society. He or she is a complete innocent and the shops, banks and others will have this poor person for breakfast if you do not help. How would you prepare such a person for their first encounter with the shops, advertising and the hard selling techniques in your nearest big shopping centre? Think of it almost like a military operation. They are out there and they want your money and your friend's money. How can you survive, so that you spend your money on what you want, not on what 'they' want you to buy?

   Stage One

   In pairs, one of you act the part of the friend from another culture and the other as yourself. Work out how you are going to get through the shopping centre and withstand the pressures to buy. Draw up your plan on paper as you will need it for the next stage.

   Stage Two

   Now change from being the shoppers to being the salespeople, shop keepers and so on. Take one role, perhaps the bank manager extending you a loan; the man on the corner selling things cheaply from a suitcase or the floor sales person trying to get people into the shop for a special bargain deal. Work out how, without going too much over the top, you would try to sell something to the two visitors.

   Stage Three

   One pair takes the role of the visitors and each of the other groups tries to sell them something. If the selling pairs come up with an idea, argument or line which the visitors had not thought of and therefore have no response to, then the sellers win.

2. Would you let someone kick you in the shins for £10? The following game is based on that idea. You have to decide what penalties people are prepared to pay in order to get money, and what pleasures people would want to pay money for.

   The class divides into three groups.

   Group One – The Customers
   You live a simple life, not very different from your real life, but you have no luxuries such as television, holidays away from home, outings, sports activities, or fashionable clothes. All your

basic needs are provided for, and you go to school for the same hours and with the same holidays as you do now. You start the game with £50 to spend.

Materials
You will need some banknotes to represent the £50. Make these out of paper before the game starts.

You will also need a penalty form each (see page 63).

Aim
Your aim is simply to make your life as happy as possible.

Procedure
When the game starts, you can buy pleasures and luxuries from the 'sellers'. Make sure you are given a token for each pleasure you buy. When your money runs out, you can get more by accepting penalties from the 'money-bags'. They will write in your penalty sheet, and you will write in their penalty sheet. At any stage you can decide that you do not want any more money or pleasures.

Group Two – The Sellers
You are selling pleasures and luxuries.

Materials
Make some tokens representing the goods you are offering for sale. These can be anything you like that you think your customers might want to buy such as a holiday at the beach, a smart jacket, the opportunity to play sports once a week, an extra week's school holiday, a good-natured teacher!

Aim
Your aim is to make as much 'money' as possible by selling pleasures to the 'customers'.

Procedure
When the game starts, you offer your pleasures for sale. You cannot change what you are selling, but you can change the price at any time. For example, if your beach holidays are more expensive than anyone else's, you will have no customers but if you charge too little you will make less money.

Group Three – The Money-Bags

You are giving money away, in exchange for various 'penalties' (imaginary, of course!) that you think people might be prepared to pay.

Materials

Make some banknotes to give out. Prepare a penalty sheet as shown.

PENALTY SHEET

Name	Penalty	Price paid

Prepare a list of what penalties you will be asking for. These can be anything that you think people will be prepared to accept in exchange for money: one week off your school holidays, the 'flu, an hour's extra homework, insufficient food, an ogre for a headteacher, etc.

Aim

Your aim is to give out as many penalties as possible.

Procedure

When the game starts, you can use any means you like to encourage the 'customers' to accept your penalties. You can describe all the good things they could buy with the money; you can persuade them that the penalties are not too bad; you can offer more money than your competitors. But if you pay too much, then the customers will be able to buy all the pleasures they want, and will not come back for any more penalties.

When you and a customer have agreed on a deal, you each fill in the other's penalty sheet, recording what penalty they have paid, and what money you gave in exchange.

The teacher will tell you how long you have for your buying and selling. At the end of that time, the customers will explain how much money they have left, what pleasures they have bought, and what penalties they have paid. They will say whether they are happy with their 'shopping', and why. The other two groups will add up how well they have done, and explain how they set about it.

Then discuss:

a) Were there any pleasures for which there was no limit to the price that customers were prepared to pay?

b) Were there any penalties which no one would accept at any price?

If you did not find any of these in the game, work in groups to produce a list of four each.

The Blast

For the first time ever – as far as Christine was concerned – the newspaper was late. She cursed and hurried through to the dining room. The TV was on for the morning news programme. Christine settled herself so she could see the TV easily, but not too obviously.

'You look as if you're expecting to hear you've won the pools,' said her dad.

'What do you mean?' replied Christine. 'Can't I watch the TV if I want to? You do.' Her father shrugged. He was not going to get into an argument this early in the day.

When at last the news item she had been waiting for came, Christine visibly sat up.

'Early this morning,' said the reporter, 'the main reception area of the Kinross Animal Experiment

Animal rights protesters blow up the car of an employee of a research laboratory

Centre was blown up. Police suspect that members of the Animal Freedom Band were responsible. The night-watchman, Mr Alfred Goddard, aged 66, was injured in the blast. The emergency unit at Kinross General Hospital says he may have to have his left leg amputated. Mr Goddard was visited this morning by his wife, daughter and his two-week-old grandson.'

Christine sat in stunned silence. This was not what she had thought would happen. How could it have gone wrong? They said no one was there at that time of night.

'Isn't that terrible?' said her father. 'Some nutcase plants a bomb and some poor old man, doing no one any harm, gets hurt. Terrible.'

'Oh come off it, John,' said her mother. 'What do you mean "doing no one any harm?" You know as well as I do what goes on in those labs. The animals are tortured there. And you know that the Peace Alliance claim biological weapons have been developed at Kinross. It's tough on the old man, but his wages have come from very dubious sources.'

'So you're saying that it's all right to blow a man's leg off if his wages are paid by an unpopular company. On that basis you could go and blow the legs off almost any night-watchman.'

Christine's mother responded briskly. 'I don't seem to recall you were worried about the use of bombs by people in South Africa who wanted to overthrow the apartheid system. Or what about the Resistance movement in the Second World War?'

'But that was different,' replied her father. 'That was a matter of life or death . . .'

'And so is this,' replied her mother.

'No,' said her father categorically. 'If you aren't careful you'll end up like the Medieval church. They justified the use of violence, as I recall, if an act of violence or a strategic war could prevent a greater act of violence or war. Fine idea when you're a small, underground movement like the early Churches. But very dangerous once you get power. Just look at the wars the Pope launched to get land and power – he called them Just Wars.'

'Dad, that's not the point,' said Christine, coming out of her silence. 'Sometimes there are wrongs which you have to protest about. No one pays any attention unless you sometimes use force. You watch, now there will be lots of programmes and debates about animal experiments. The means may be violent, but the end justifies them. If we can stop cruelty to animals and the development of biological weapons by a few bombs, the whole world will be a better place.'

Christine spoke these words with real conviction. This was because she had believed them when she first heard them. Unknown to her parents, she belonged to a local group, or 'cell' of the Animal Freedom Band. Two weeks ago they had been told of the coming attack on 'a major centre of animal torture'. No name had been given for security reasons. But Christine had learned later which date the attack would take place. She had given £5 to help pay for the costs because she believed that such action was right.

'Do you really believe that the victory of goodness can be achieved by evil?' asked her father. 'If the pro-animal people have been telling you this, it's rubbish.'

'But I thought you supported the use of violence to defend yourself and those you love,' said Christine. 'That's what you told me once when I wanted to become a pacifist.'

'But only in very special situations,' replied her father.

'Oh, come on,' answered her mother. 'We're not talking about something like one of those Muslim Holy Wars, or the Crusades. We're talking about shocking people into looking at why they do the things they do in the hope that they will change. I'll bet far fewer people will buy goods tested on animals as a result of that bomb blast and the discussion it creates.'

'But,' said her father, 'there are non-violent means. Take Greenpeace. They don't blow people up but they do things, organise demonstrations and so on which make people sit up and take notice.'

'Yes, but sometimes,' argued Christine, 'sometimes a bit more of a push is needed.'

'Well tell that to the poor watchman,' retorted her father. 'I expect he will need to be pushed around in a wheelchair for the rest of his life.'

At this, Christine turned white and ran from the room.

'Now what have I said?' asked her father, but her mother had put two and two together and was already heading up the stairs to talk to her.

Information box

Animal Rights

During the last 30 years there has been a growing international movement to protect animals who are killed or suffer needlessly for sport or to provide luxuries such as fur. The movement also fights for the rights of animals who are used during the testing of drugs or cosmetics.

Religions have always expressed a concern for animals in their teachings and there have always been individuals or groups who have cared for the welfare of animals. At the same time many concerned people felt that the public knew very little about the way that animals were used in laboratories or the means by which they were hunted or killed. They believed that by forming organised groups the laws of the country would change so that animals can be protected from suffering to some extent.

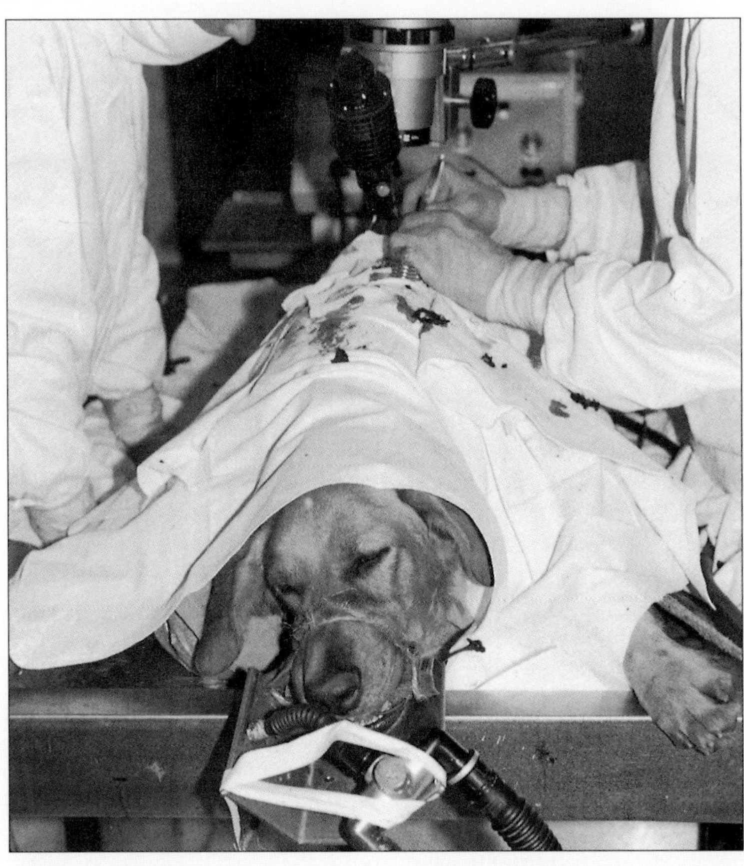

Dog being operated on at a department of animal experimentation

Not everyone agrees with the claims of the animal rights protesters and not all of the animal rights or protection groups agree with each other. Some try to attract public notice to the use of animals by planting bombs or attacking buildings. Most of the animal rights and protection groups, however, try to carry out their work through education and other peaceful means.

Activities

Work out the following two drama scenes:

1. a) The meeting of the Animal Freedom Band 'cell' which Christine attended. Argue for and against the use of the bomb attack.

   b) What Christine's mum would have said to Christine and Christine's reply when her mum asked her outright if she had anything to do with the attack.

2. What other examples of violence in a just cause are mentioned in the story?

   Take one and find out more about it. What was the situation? What violent action was taken?

The Crusades

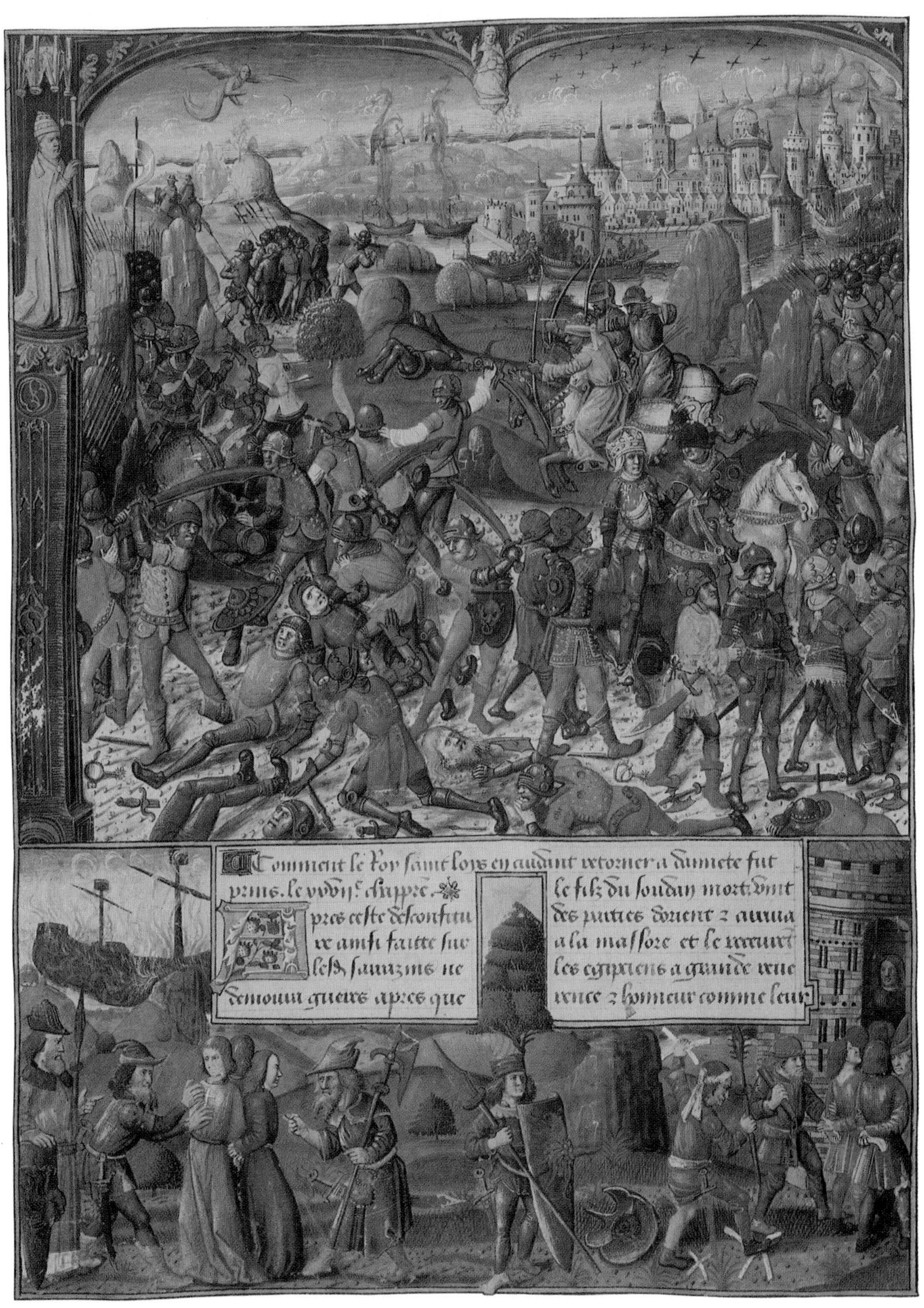

The Muslim soldiers could not believe their eyes. At first they thought it was the glare from the desert sands which was affecting their eyesight. Then they saw that two men were walking towards them. 'Well, someone go and catch them,' said the commander of the watch. 'How can we 'catch' people who are walking straight towards us, sir?' asked one of the soldiers. 'Don't argue with me, just go and fetch them,' replied the commander.

Meanwhile, the two men walked on. Both were dressed in simple brown robes; both were Christians and both had left the Christian camp that morning and had walked across the no-man's-land between the Christian and Muslim armies, in the summer of 1219. Their names were Illuminato and Francis of Assisi, who later became known as St Francis, the founder of the Franciscan order. But what were they doing walking into the Muslim camp?

To understand this we need to go back to Francis' youth. He was a wild young man and a soldier. As a young man he longed to go on the Crusades. What could be greater, he thought, than to fight for Christ against the heathen Muslims who had seized the Holy Places of Jerusalem. Like most of his generation, Francis had grown up being told by the Church that to fight against the Muslims was to do God's work. Then, Francis changed his way of life. He gave up being a soldier and became a wandering teacher and worker for God. But still he longed to go to the Crusades. He saw them as glorious battles fought by the shining knights of Christianity against the evil forces of the Saracens. He saw the Christian troops as the army of good against the army of evil.

So he came with Brother Illuminato, to see the Crusades in action. But it was not what he expected. He found the Christian army to have very few shining knights or good Christian souls. They were a vicious army with internal disagreements and disputes. He saw them attack helpless villages and he realised that there was no such thing as a Holy War.

What should he do? He still hoped that the Holy Places of Jerusalem could be Christian again, but he saw that the armies fighting in the Crusades were not the way. Even if the Pope had told them they were fighting for Jesus, Francis saw that they were really fighting for money and adventure.

So one night, he and Brother Illuminato decided to try to convert the Muslims to Christianity, not by force of arms, but by preaching. The plan sounded foolhardy, but it risked no lives except their own. Francis and Illuminato had just watched the Christian army retreat after they were badly beaten from an attack on the Muslim army. Thousands had died that day in the hot sun of the border land of Egypt and Palestine. Francis wanted no more death.

The Muslim soldiers soon surrounded the two monks and led them to the Muslim camp where they became prisoners. But the Muslims did not know what to do with them. Like the Christians, they had been taught that there was such a thing as a Holy War. A jihad or justified war can only be started by Muslims in order to help spread Islam. Before such a Holy War starts, however, the enemy must have been offered a genuine chance to become Muslims without use of war. If they refuse or threaten Islam in any way, then Islam teaches that it is the duty of Muslims to fight to bring the whole world under Islam. Islam also teaches that anyone who dies in a Holy War, will go straight to paradise. This idea was adopted by the Popes who, when they declared a Holy War against Islam, told the Christian soldiers that they would go straight to heaven if they were killed fighting the Muslims.

The Muslims did not know what to do with two preachers who had voluntarily come into their camp. Finally, news of them reached the leader of the army. The Sultan al-Kamil asked about the monks and was told that anyone so simple, so gentle and so honest as these two, was obviously touched by God and so worthy of being listened to. The Sultan himself wanted peace. So Francis and Illuminato came before the Sultan and spoke about their beliefs and urged the Sultan to accept Christ. The Sultan refused, but very politely. So Francis then asked for a truce, so that peace talks could begin. The Sultan agreed to this. He sent Francis and Illuminato back to the Christian camp with a special guard and with offers of many gifts which Francis politely refused. The Sultan and Francis seemed to have got on very well. Both could see the folly of the 'Holy War' which they and their fellow believers were involved in. Sadly, the truce lasted only a short time and the terrible wars of the Holy Land dragged on for many more years. But neither side quite forgot that Francis and the Sultan had shown that there was another way for people of different faiths to meet.

Information box

St Francis

St Francis of Assisi was the son of a wealthy merchant from the town of Assisi in Italy. When he was a teenager Francis was inspired by the tales of courage, adventure and honour that he heard from the knights who fought for Christianity in the Crusades. So he decided to join them. On the first day of his journey to join the Crusaders, Francis heard a mysterious voice telling him to return to Assisi. Francis believed this to be the voice of God and felt that he must obey this request. The voice spoke to him several times again and shortly after, to everyone's surprise, he gave up the life of riches and comfort.

St Francis by Zurbaran

He committed himself to a life of poverty and humility so that he could preach about the Kingdom of God and repentance. Francis was committed to a life of peace and caring for all living things since they were part of God's creation. At first his family and friends thought he was mad as he wandered the streets and towns begging and praying, wearing only a coarse robe. But gradually, other men and women, mainly from wealthy families, joined him. When Francis did go to the Crusades later in his life it was to proclaim peace, not war.

Activities

1. Write a conversation between Francis and the Sultan where each explains what his faith says about fighting, and why his army is fighting.
2. What would people in the Christian camp have said to Francis if he had told them of his plan?
3. What would people in the Muslim camp have said to someone who had a similar idea on their side?
4. Do you think a war can be justified? Look at wars or crises that are in the news. What are the reasons for them? Try to find out the arguments on each side.

Sources

CHRISTIANITY

Fundamentally, Christianity is opposed to violence and warfare. However, this basic position has many variations. The main churches – Roman Catholic, Orthodox and most of the Protestant churches believe that in a completely Christian world, war would be totally forbidden in the light of Jesus' teaching in Matthew 5–7. However, most churches accept that they live in a world of conflicting powers and they have long taught that under certain circumstances war is justified. For instance, the Roman Catholic Church has set forth four basic conditions for Christians to participate justly in a war:

1. It must be done on the authority of a ruler
2. The cause must be just – such as the overthrow of a dictator
3. Those taking part must do so for good and just reasons, not for personal profit, glory or benefit
4. The war must be carried out by proper means. This means not attacking civilians, or using weapons which destroy everything, such as nuclear weapons or chemical warfare.

While this covers the bulk of Christians (including many who have joined revolutions or struggles against oppression such as apartheid) there are some churches and Christian groups who are completely pacifist. Two very famous such groups are the Mennonites (named after their first leader Menno Simons, 1496–1561) and the Society of Friends (Quakers) founded in the mid-seventeenth century.

In 1660 the Quakers produced a document called 'A Declaration from the Harmless and Innocent People of God called Quakers'. It sets out the principles which the Quakers have upheld ever since.

BUDDHISM

Buddhists vow to do their best to refrain from killing and other violence. To the enlightened, all life is interconnected and as one. To injure another would be like cutting off your left hand with your right. Everything possible should be done to avoid it by mediation, compromise, reconciliation, and non-violent action of various kinds.

However, only when we become aware of the roots of violence within ourselves can we work in a truly effective and non-violent way towards ending the violence of others.

Buddhism recognises that situations arise in the lives of individuals and the history of nations where it is unclear how to act for the best. Buddhism provides guidelines for right action but at the same time acknowledges that the people concerned must make the final decision, after calm and careful reflection. And they must take full responsibility for the consequences of that decision. This requires much courage, for the fragile, insecure self desperately feels the need to be always in the right.

JUDAISM

The aim of Judaism is peace and this is expressed throughout the Jewish tradition. When one Jew greets another he or she usually says 'Shalom Uleichem' – Peace unto you. The word 'Shalom' derives from a root meaning 'to be whole' and in this greeting there is the notion that peace comes from a wholeness of a personality.

Jews do not believe in a holy war since war is the destruction of human life and that cannot be holy. Jews are not pacifists: they are entitled to take up arms for the defence of themselves and their children and such wars may be justified. Jews believe in the pursuit of peace through science, law, medicine, the arts and agriculture.

JAINISM

'Ahimso Parmo Dharma' – Non-violence is the supreme religion – is the first and most important teaching of the Jain faith. All other teachings follow from this.

The principle of 'ahimsa', non-violence, requires Jains to take great care not to harm any form of life, from the microscopic beings believed to fill the universe to other human beings.

The Jain tirthankara (saint), Mahavir, who lived 2 500 years ago in India said 'Nobody likes suffering. Therefore do not inflict suffering on anybody. This is non-violence, this is equality' (Sutra Kratanga).

All beings are believed to have souls and all have the potential to become God when they have achieved absolute 'ahimsa' – non-violence. This means that when a person is violent towards another, they are violent against themselves, because they are preventing their soul from reaching the ultimate bliss of Moksha.

Vegetarianism is considered a basic and powerful practice of non-violence and is practised by nearly all Jains. Certain foods that are believed to have large quantities of microscopic beings living in them, such as onions, garlic, ginger, alcohol and figs, are also left out of the Jain diet. Filtering water to take out the small lifeforms before drinking it is normal practice in Jain households. The evening meal is cooked before sunset so that the insects are not attracted by the light of the cooking fires and fly to their death.

Jains avoid occupations such as hunting, fishing or the timber industry. They often work in business but avoid dealing with occupations which cause harm to others such as weapons, timber, livestock or animal by-products, excavation and mining.

Jain saddhi and saddhus (nuns and monks) are even more strict in their care not to harm any forms of life. They carry whisk brooms to sweep away small insects in their path and they wear masks across their mouths so they will not inadvertently swallow any insects or other small creatures.

Jains are expected to practise non-violence not only in speech and deed but also in thought. In fact non-violent thought is the most important because it is violent thought that creates violent speech and action. If a doctor accidently kills a patient while operating to save her life that would be a great tragedy but it would not be a violent act because the intention was not to kill.

'Ahimso parma dharma' means that for a soul to become divine it must lose all its attachments, because only then is it truly non-violent.

ISLAM

Amongst all the precepts of Islam, it is perhaps Jihad which is most often misquoted and misused. The word itself means literally 'to strive in the way of Allah'. Contrary to popular belief, it does not mean 'holy war'. A person who strives in this way is called a Mujahid.

Muslims believe war can be justified in certain circumstances such as in self-defence, to fight oppression and against injustice. The Qur'an and the sayings of Prophet Muhammad are explicit about not only when war is permissible but also how it should be conducted.

Nuclear weapons and other weapons which kill indiscriminately are to be abhorred, if for no other reason than the fact that innocent people are inevitably going to suffer from their use. Since the Prophet's advice included that not a tree should be cut down or an animal slain by a Muslim army, it is easy to see that Muslims believe that you should only fight against those who are fighting you without damaging (if at all possible) the surrounding environment. Civil war is equally bound by the conditions covering other wars and it is a great sin for a Muslim to kill a fellow Muslim without a just reason.

The Qur'an makes it clear that killing of any kind is only permissible in strictly controlled circumstances; hence murder is a capital offence and is harshly punished, unless the victim's family forgives the murderer and asks for a lesser punishment than death.

Any loss of life is to be regretted, but if it is done in the true spirit of justice, according to the laws of Allah given in the Qur'an and the sayings of the Prophet Muhammad, then it must be accepted.

Role-play

1. In the story of the Animal Freedom Band, Christine genuinely believed that what she was doing was right. The situation you now have to play out is that she and the others responsible have been caught and are on trial. You are the jury and each of you belongs to a specific religion. You have heard all the evidence (reread the story) and you have now been sent to judge the case and to decide whether Christine and her friends should be imprisoned.

   Divide the class into religious groups based on the information on the previous pages. Each group must then discuss what they think their verdict should be, based upon the faith's teaching. Then bring the class together again and allow each faith to give its verdict and the reasons why it has made this decision. Add together the results and see if your jury sends Christine and the others to gaol.

2. Imagine that you are living at the time of the Crusades. Although it is the thirteenth century before printing had been invented, there are newspapers published by the different religions and groups. Write up the story of the Crusades from the point of view of any one of the following newspapers and remember to think of popular style banner headlines and key words which you could highlight in the text. The newspapers which need to have you as a reporter are:
   - The Quaker Times
   - The Islamic Herald
   - Crusader's Weekly
   - The Jewish Post
   - Buddhist Star.

The Hostel

Most people claimed that the first they knew about it was when they read *The Advertiser*, the local free newspaper. The article caught the attention of everybody.

'Down-and-outs hostel to be built in residential area – outrage.' If there was not an outrage before the article appeared, there certainly was afterwards.

'The Salvation Army has announced plans, apparently approved by the town council, to build a 50-room hostel for drunks, drug addicts and other down-and-outs,' said the paper. The Salvation Army were furious to see how the paper described those it intended to help. But they were soon at the centre of a terrible row.

A local Action Committee sprang up to 'fight this invasion of our homes and the threat it poses to our children.' Soon posters appeared and people and shops were pressurised to display them. The posters were quite frightening. They showed a little girl cowering in a corner as a huge, obviously drunk tramp towered over her with a broken bottle. This proved too much for the local clergy. In an open letter they sent to *The Advertiser*, they pointed out how cruel and inaccurate both the poster and the campaign were.

'The Salvation Army wishes to build a hostel where people, many of whom are ordinary men and women like you or us, can live. These people have been hurt by life. Some have been on drugs, others on alcohol. But they are now trying to rebuild their lives. They deserve a chance. We should be proud that we can help them.'

But it seemed to do little good. New posters appeared. 'No strangers here', 'Protect our children from strangers' and other such emotional statements. The vicar's car was spray-painted with the words 'Drug Dealer' and the Salvation Army office received obscene telephone calls and threatening letters.

Ironically, it was the very children whom the Action Committee said they were protecting who brought the thing to a head. It began as a discussion in class when Alison said how disgusted she was by the campaign. 'This community is sick,' she claimed. 'We must help these people – not try and turn them away. Did you hear what one of the members of the Committee said yesterday? "Let somewhere else look after them – but not us." It's sick. I really admire the Vicar for what he has said, but why don't others stand up with him?' And that, coming from Alison, was praise indeed.

Well, debate broke out. In the end, Mr Coustins, their PSE teacher, agreed to raise the issue with the Head. Meanwhile, others in the class agreed to ask their parents and where appropriate, religious leaders, what they thought.

A day later the Headmistress was inviting the Salvation Army, the local clergy and the Action Committee to hold an open meeting a week later to discuss the proposed hostel. By the time of the meeting the list had grown. Amongst those invited were the Salvation Army, the Vicar, Imam Nasseef, Rabbi Schwartz, the President of the Sikh Temple, Mr K Singh and the Chair of the local council. Also present were the Action Committee, the local traders' committee and the Rotary Club. But the first to speak were the 'Build the hostel – welcome the strangers' Committee of children at the school.

'We should be proud to have such a hostel,' said Alison at the start of the meeting. 'There are many people in this town who need help. Just because they don't live in this area, doesn't mean they don't exist. I'm not frightened at the thought of these people coming to live in a hostel in our area. I'm much more frightened to think what might happen to them and perhaps to me if they don't have a hostel like the one that is planned.'

Mr Banks, the Chairman of the Action Committee replied. 'Of course people like these need help. We all agree on that. But this is not the right place. We cannot be sure how they will behave. They may be recovering – but what if they go back on drugs or alcohol? Do we want to run the risk of such strangers attacking us in our own area; making noise, disturbances or giving visitors to the area a bad impression? I don't think so – and think what it will do to house prices in the area. They will fall.'

So the debate got off to a lively start.

Information box

The Salvation Army

The Salvation Army are a group of Christians who raise money for, and work with, the homeless, destitute and sick in towns and cities throughout the world. The Salvation Army was founded in England by William Booth in 1865. It is organised on military lines, with a general at the head and members see themselves as an army working for Christ. Members try to follow Christ's teachings as closely as possible in everything they do. They do not build their own churches since their aim is to bring religion to all people. They spread the Word of God through their work and prayer and also through their music which is played by the famous Salvation Army brass bands.

Salvation Army hand out sleeping bags, soup and bread

Activities

1. Much of the argument in the story is about where certain people 'belong'. Are there places where you do not 'belong', either because people do not welcome you or because you feel different from them? For example, a place where everyone is a different age from you, or has different interests, or speaks with a different accent. Describe this place, and the people who go there.
2. Look at the information and write a brief speech for each of the following people at the meeting described in the story: the Vicar, the Imam; the Rabbi; the Sikh President and the traders' committee.
3. Take a vote on what you think would have been the decision of the meeting.

Ruth

Naomi felt the grief and fear and loneliness sweep over her. She had come many years before as a stranger in a strange land to make a new life. Times were bad at home, so she had set out with her husband and two sons to where there was a better chance for the family to thrive. At first things were difficult. The people and their customs were strange, and even the gods were different. But her husband had worked hard and the family settled down and made a life for themselves.

But then Naomi's husband died, leaving her with her two sons. But her sons were nearly grown up by this time, and they too worked hard and looked after their mother. In time, they both married local girls, and Naomi became very fond of her daughters-in-law, and began to feel that she belonged here after all. But then tragedy struck. Both her sons died. The loving care of her daughters-in-law, Ruth and Orpah, could not bring her any comfort.

'You, my daughters, have a life here,' she said. 'But now that my husband and my sons are dead, there is nothing more for me here. Go back to your families, and find new husbands. May the Lord be as kind to you as you have been to me and to those who have died. But I will go back to my homeland of Israel. Times are better there now, there is no more famine, and I will make my life amongst my own people.'

But Ruth and Orpah clung to her all the more, and wept as they said, 'You have been a mother to us, and we will not leave you. We will come with you to your people.'

'No,' said Naomi, 'you must go back. I am old, I have nothing to give you. I cannot find husbands for you. I have no more sons, and I am too old to marry again. Go back to your people.'

'You are right,' said Orpah. 'I love you dearly, but I had better go back to my own family.' And she kissed Naomi, and returned to her own mother's house. But Ruth stayed with Naomi, and would not leave.

'Look,' said Naomi, 'your sister-in-law has seen sense and has returned to her family. You must do the same. Leave me.'

But Ruth said, 'Do not urge me to leave you. For wherever you go, I will go; wherever you live, I will live. Your people shall be my people, and your God shall be my God. Wherever you die, I will die, and there I will be buried.'

Seeing that she was so determined, Naomi said no more, and together they set out for the land of Israel, to Naomi's home town of Bethlehem.

Their arrival caused a lot of talk. 'Fancy Naomi coming back here after all these years!' said the women. 'And who is that foreign woman who's come back with her?'

Now it was Ruth's turn to be a stranger in a strange land. It was the time of the barley harvest, and every day cheerful parties of women and girls set off for the fields to glean – to pick up the corn that the farm workers had left. Anything they picked up they could keep. Ruth also went out into the fields to glean, but there was no chattering group for her to join. She was the stranger, and she was left alone to work. No one mistreated her, but no one made any attempt to make friends.

But Boaz, the owner of the fields, was a kind and just man. He saw the lonely figure in the fields and asked about her. 'Oh, that's the woman from Moab, who came back with Naomi. She came to ask if she could glean, and she's been on her feet picking up corn from morning till now,' he was told.

'Look after her,' said Boaz, 'and make sure she gets something to eat and drink.' And to Ruth he said, 'You are welcome to come and glean my fields. Don't go to other farms where you might be mistreated, but come here to my fields every day, and my workers will make sure no one gives you any trouble.'

All through the barley harvest and all through the wheat harvest, Ruth gleaned in the fields of Boaz. As the days went by, Boaz learned more of Ruth's faithfulness and love for Naomi and Ruth learnt more of Boaz's justice, fairness and kindness. And when the barley was on the threshing-floor and the wheat lay in heaps in Boaz's barns, Boaz asked Ruth to marry him.

So Ruth, the immigrant, made her home in Israel. And it was not long after that Ruth and Boaz had a son. 'Blessed be the Lord who has not left you without descendants!' said the women to Naomi. 'Your sons have died, but this child will be the comfort and joy of your old age, for your daughter-in-law who loves you and has been more to you than seven sons, has given him birth.'

And it was through this child, Obed, that Ruth became the great-grandmother of the king of Israel. For Obed had a son, Jesse, and Jesse's son was none other than the great King David, the greatest king that the people of Israel have ever known.

Activities

1. Ruth decided not to go back to her own family, but to stay with Naomi, even though it meant going to a strange land. Imagine you are Ruth, and write a letter to your family telling them of your decision. Try to explain your reasons.
2. The story of Ruth comes from the Bible. In the Bible, many stories tell us that people sang songs or wrote poems when important things happened to them. Write a song or a poem for one of the characters in this story, at a time when something sad or something good happens to them: for example, when Naomi's sons died; when Naomi's grandson was born; when Ruth left her own country; when Ruth married Boaz; and so on. Use some of the words from the story if you like, or some words from the book of Ruth in the Bible, but use some of your own words as well.
3. Boaz was one of the few people who made Ruth welcome when she first arrived in Israel. If the story happened now, in your area, who might make Ruth welcome? What could you do to help?
4. There are many difficulties in settling into a new country. List as many of them as you can think of. Against each one, write down what other people might do to help.

Sources

CHRISTIANITY

The idea of caring for the stranger is deeply rooted in Christianity and especially in the teachings and stories of Jesus. The most important of Jesus' teachings on this is found in Matthew 25, where he tells the story of the sheep and the goats. Here people are rewarded or punished depending on whether they cared for Jesus when he was sick, hungry, poor, naked or in prison. When people say 'But we never saw you', Jesus replies that whenever you help a stranger, you help him. This teaching is strongly reinforced by the story of the Good Samaritan.

Hospitality to travellers is a tradition of most monasteries both in the past and today. The stranger is seen not only as someone who needs help, but as Christ himself. Folk legends about Jesus not being recognised but being treated hospitably are very common in Christianity; for example, look up the story of Papa Panov in Russia as retold by Tolstoy.

BUDDHISM

There are many stories of how the Buddha scandalised people by inviting outcasts and untouchables to join his followers. One such 'untouchable', whose work was confined to the filthiest of jobs, replied in delight and astonishment, 'Sir, no one has ever spoken kindly to me. Usually I am just ordered about and hardly noticed.'

On another occasion when he was teaching, the Buddha noticed a poor and hungry man who had crept in at the back of the crowd. He refused to continue until the man had been fed. Some people complained about this interruption, but the Buddha explained that 'If I had preached to this man while he was hungry he would not have been able to follow me. There is no affliction like the affliction of hunger.'

HINDUISM

In Hindu culture one of the best things you can do is to receive the unexpected visitor. Many families will make a practice of inviting poor people in and feeding them, and this is still done in India. A householder should not take his or her meal without first seeing if there is anyone hungry. They should call three times on the road, 'Is anyone hungry?'

Indulgence in certain types of behaviour such as eating meat, excessive drinking, and adultery are frowned upon by Hindus and can result in being rejected from society.

JUDAISM

For thousands of years the Jewish people have followed the example of their founding father, Abraham, by showing their hospitality to the stranger, the lonely and the rejected. Before the Jews were expelled from Egypt, after the Destruction of the Temple in AD 70, many householders set out small flags at meal times as a sign to the poor and hungry that food was being served and that they were welcome as guests. In the Talmud, a collection of special religious writings, Jews are expected to treat the stranger as an honoured guest. The quality or quantity of the food was not important but it was important how much effort the host put into caring for his guests. Even children were taught how to treat the poor and needy with respect, to welcome them into the home and to lay food before them.

Jewish hospitality was much needed during the Middle Ages and onwards when Jews suffered many persecutions. Those who were made homeless or who were escaping persecution could rely on Jewish families in other cities or lands to show them hospitality by providing shelter and food. During the Middle Ages it became the custom for Jews, after attending the synagogue service on Friday evening, to invite strangers for the Sabbath. The guest could draw warmth and reassurance from the family circle. In this way they fulfilled the teachings in the Mishnah, the book of Oral Laws: 'Let the poor be members of your household.'

ISLAM

The Prophet Muhammad said 'He who believes in Allah and the Last Day should honour his guest.'

Guests and travellers have a special place in Islam, and hospitality is a very important duty. This was illustrated very early in the history of Islam, when many Muslims fled from the persecution in Makkah, and settled in Medina. They arrived in Medina with no possessions, but the Muslims there took them into their homes and looked after them. When Muhammad also left Makkah for Medina, he held a meeting for the residents of Medina and the newly arrived refugees. He suggested that they should all become brothers and share their property and other belongings. The original residents of Medina agreed to this, and their generosity to those arriving in their city has been an example for Muslims ever since.

Role-play

1. Strangers come to your area everyday. They need to know how to find things, how to travel around, where to shop and so forth. You are 'locals' and you know the area. The aim of this role-play is to try to see your area through the eyes of a stranger. Divide into two groups; one group will be the strangers. Think about what you usually want to know when you visit somewhere. What sort of things in your area would seem odd or confusing to a stranger? What information do you need to have?

The second group has to think of the advice it needs to provide for strangers. So you have to think about the things which you think they would find odd, strange or confusing. Compile a set of basic information sheets on these topics.

Then bring both groups together. Find out to what extent the questions the 'stranger' group have asked are answered by the 'locals' group. What issues did you agree upon; what issues did each group think of which the other did not? How much have you learned about the strangeness of your own area? What suggestions do you have for your local council/tourist board, etc., which might be helpful to strangers?

2. Many police forces are having to find ways in which to tell young children to be careful of strangers.

There are several problems with this. They need to decide:

- Who is a stranger?
- Should we be teaching children to be afraid of anybody that they do not know?
- How are strangers to become accepted in a new place if everyone is wary of them?

Divide into groups representing the police, community workers, teachers, young people's representatives, and members of different religions who are going to come together to decide what to do. Prepare the arguments you would use in these different groups. Once you have done this, come together with the rest of the class and present your different cases. Can you arrive at an agreed way to proceed which takes into account the fear of children being hurt and the fact that all strangers need not be feared?

Once you have arrived at such a document, send it to your local police force to get their reaction.

What the Papers Say

Colin was early. The newspapers were laid out ready except for the TV Times. He had to wait for that before setting off on his paper round. This gave him the excuse to flick through the papers.

Jerusalem and the area to the east of the city had had a sharp downpour of rain the day before. Avi Weisburg was driving to work when it rained. An ambitious young man, he was on his way to sell a life insurance policy to a family who had just settled into a new town in the Israeli occupied territories outside Jerusalem. His car, however, was not working properly. The windscreen wipers only worked every now and then, so Avi slowed the car down. That is when they attacked. Avi never saw them. He had driven through an Arab village and was just beginning the climb up the hill to the Jewish settlement when the first stone hit the windscreen. The glass cracked but did not break. Avi panicked. He lost control and crashed down the side of the road into a gully. He died when his head struck the top of the car.

An hour later, Abul Halim was walking home from school. Unfortunately for him, he took a short cut down the long alley that runs from the mosque to the market. He heard the riot before he saw it. As he neared the end of the alley by the market, a gang of young Arab men ran towards him. He knew some of them. Following quickly behind were the Israeli soldiers. The gang ran past, leaving Abul exposed. He raised his hand as if to say 'I'm nothing to do with this.' But the young, very frightened Israeli soldier did not understand. Later he told the Court, 'I thought he had a stone in his hand. I thought he was defying me, standing there so calm and cool. I couldn't stand it. So I fired. I'm so sorry.'

Abul never really felt the bullet. He was buried with his satchel of books.

Colin scanned the papers. On the international news page of one of the quality papers, he read about the murder of Avi Weisburg, 'a promising young man'. At the end of the article, the paper noted that two Arabs were shot dead in the Occupied Territories yesterday, bringing the total to 150 Arabs killed so far this year. They did not name Abul.

In another country in Africa, death walked again. An American official with Oxfam was killed when her landrover hit a landmine planted by guerillas fighting the government. It was a tragic loss. 50 miles away a girl died. She was 13 years old. Her death was caused by gangrene setting in to a leg shattered by a landmine. She was one of 15 children who died in the same refugee camp that day.

Colin's eye was caught by a photograph of the American woman in one of the more popular papers. 'Good Samaritan killed in mercy mission dash' said the headline. Colin thought what a shame it was that such a nice looking young woman should have died in such a sad way. He never heard about the 13-year-old girl or the other 14 children who died that day.

The four friends had planned this holiday for some time. They flew to Spain and hired a car at the airport. George had always said that Nancy drove too fast, but as the others pointed out, she had never had an accident yet. So Nancy drove. The bus was probably at fault. It was too far over on the wrong side of the road and Nancy could not have avoided it, even if she had been going more slowly. As it was she tried her best, but it was useless. The other couple survived. George and Nancy were dead on arrival at the local hospital.

On the same day in Pakistan, the ferry across the Indus river was full. There were the usual crowd of families, business people, farmers returning home, and students and people just going to visit friends and relations. Among them was the Khan family. There were six of them, Mr and Mrs Khan and their four daughters. They were returning from a family wedding. At long last, Uncle Omar had got married! It had been a grand wedding. Now they were going home. They did not know that a

ferocious tropical rainstorm had burst on the river 30 miles away. The first – and for many the last – they knew of it was when the tidal wave swept round the bend of the river, hitting the ferry sideways on. The ferry sank almost instantly. Boats rushed out from both sides of the river but at the end of the day 52 men, women and children were drowned.

Colin glanced at the front page of a paper noted for its foreign news coverage. The front page told the story of George and Nancy's death and also showed a photograph of the wrecked car. At the bottom was a brief paragraph about the ferry boat that sunk in Pakistan. It did not mention who died, just that a freak tidal wave caused the death of over 50 people.

Colin tidied up the papers. 'Dangerous to go abroad,' he thought to himself. When Gavin came in, he asked 'Anything interesting in the papers today?'

'No,' said Colin, 'just the usual old stuff,' as he and Gavin went on their daily newspaper round.

Activities

1. Why do you think that George and Nancy were named in the newspaper and the Khan family were not? There may be several reasons, some good and some bad.
2. Collect several different newspapers, both tabloids and broadsheets. Cut out any items which cover events outside Europe. Divide these into different sorts of events, such as trade news, diplomatic news, war news, and so on. Make a list of any people mentioned. On one side of the page list those mentioned by name and on the other side those who were not named. Where possible, write down their nationality. Is there a difference between your two lists? If so, why do you think this is?
3. Use the same collection of news reports. Choose the one you find the most interesting and readable, and the one you find the least interesting. What are the differences between them? Is it in:
   - the type of event covered?
   - the way it is told?
   - whether there is some 'human interest'?
   - other differences?

Remembering the Past

A pro-independence demonstration by Tibetans in Lhasa

It was swift and brutal. One moment the old Tibetan monk was standing with the banner in his hands and the next he was knocked to the ground and taken away in the police van. Few people saw what happened, and those that did turned away in fear. They thought that only a brave fool would try to interfere with the Chinese police. They all agreed with what the banner had said, but none dared say so. The banner said 'Chinese friends, please do not destroy us.'

At the police station, the old monk sat nursing his battered and bloodstained head. He was a fragile old man and the old Chinese police sergeant on duty took pity on him. He brought him some cotton to clean his wound. The police station was full of policemen. It was rumoured that a big demonstration against Chinese rule in Tibet was going to take place that afternoon near the old Dalai Lama's palace in Lhasa. The policemen quickly left the station to go to the demonstration to ensure that it did not get out of hand. A young policeman, the old sergeant and the wounded monk were the only ones left.

It was the monk who spoke first. 'Thank you for the cotton. I did not expect such kindness. What will happen to me?'

The old sergeant looked sideways at the young policeman, who was busy writing. The sergeant moved over to sit beside the monk. 'What did you do that for? Why did you go to the temple to protest? You must have known that we would stop you. Now I don't know what they will do to you.'

The old monk lowered his eyes and began to pray. The young man looked up and laughed. 'You think prayers will help you, old man? That's the trouble with you Tibetans, you're like savages. Uncivilised and clinging to old-fashioned superstitions. You Tibetans don't deserve to exist. You're freaks from the past and the sooner you're gone the better.' He spoke with such hatred that even the old monk, long used to being abused by the Chinese, looked up in surprise.

The monk had been already middle-aged when the Chinese overthrew the religious ruler of Tibet, the Dalai Lama in 1959. As a young man, the monk had visited China in the 1920s and 1930s.

'Where do you come from, my son?' he asked the young policeman. 'Are you from Shanghai?' Taken off guard by such a question, the young man replied that he was from Shanghai.

'I was there a number of times – before the revolution,' said the old monk. 'Do you know there was a park there which the Europeans had in their area? It had a sign which said "No dogs or Chinese allowed in". The Europeans used to treat the Chinese people very badly even though they were in China! I used to get very angry. But Chinese friends said that one day the Europeans would learn to treat the Chinese with respect. Then I visited Shanghai during the Japanese occupation in the Second World War. The Japanese treated the Chinese worse than the Europeans. They turned the Chinese people into slaves. If a Japanese soldier was killed by the Chinese Resistance, the Japanese would wipe out entire villages. But my friends were still hopeful. "One day," they said, "one day we shall throw out the Japanese and China will be proud again and the world will take notice." I prayed for that day, for as a Buddhist monk I have compassion for all who suffer, and the Chinese suffered under racist and imperialist rule. It is a terrible thing to be ruled by people who hate you just because you are not the same as them.'

The young policeman nodded his agreement and then suddenly realised what the old monk had said. Anger rose in him again, but this time mixed with confusion. It was the older policeman whose face registered the deepest impact of the old monk's words. Suddenly he seemed to make his mind up about something. He reached up to lift down the keys to the handcuffs on the old monk.

Who knows if he really would have let him go? For at that moment the doors swung open and in came the rest of the police force, pushing and shoving a group of Tibetan protesters. In the confusion, everything was forgotten, and the old monk was never seen again.

Information boxes

Tibet

In 1950, Chinese troops from the newly Communist state of China invaded Tibet in order to 'liberate' it. They did not immediately set about destroying the Tibetan culture. They tried to run Tibet through the old Tibetan structures. In 1959, certain Tibetan tribes rebelled and tried to throw the Chinese out. The revolt was brutally crushed. Many Tibetans were killed fighting for their independence and thousands of Tibetans, led by the Dalai Lama, their political and social leader, fled into northern India to find refuge. Chinese troops are still in Tibet and it is ruled from the Chinese capital, Beijing. Tibetans are still struggling to regain their independence and

Tibet *continued*

still regard the Dalai Lama as their true leader. He and his followers are now based at Daramasala in the foothills of the Himalayas. Although the Chinese government have asked the Dalai Lama to return to Tibet, he has refused to return until his people are free from Chinese rule. Tibet now has so many non-Tibetans living there that Tibetans are now a minority in their own country. In the late 1960s and early 1970s most of the Tibetan religious culture was destroyed and millions died. The Tibetan language was forbidden. Life is still very, very difficult for Tibetans who claim that the Chinese want to destroy their culture.

Ruins of a Tibetan monastery

Martial Law in Tibet

This is an extract from an Amnesty International Report:

'. . . during the year since the 7 March 1989 imposition of martial law in Lhasa, the capital of the Tibetan Automonous Region of the People's Republic of China, Tibetans have continued to be detained for peacefully exercising their right to hold and express opinions. Over 1,000 people were believed to be arrested in the days after martial law was declared and in subsequent months. It is impossible to maintain contact with many who are held in detention without charge or trial. Some, including prisoners of conscience, are known to have been sentenced to periods of imprisonment through administrative proceedings without a charge or trial while others were sentenced after trials that fell short of international standards of fairness. Torture and ill-treatment have continued to be reported in use in at least three of Lhasa's prisons and detention centres.'

Activities

1. There are several different examples in the story of one nation mistreating another. Make a list of them.
2. Brainstorm in class to add other examples to this list, from history or in the world today.
3. Write what the young policeman would have said when he went home and told his family what had happened. Would he have changed his mind about Tibetans?

The Rabbi in the Tower

The young rabbi stood with his head bowed in prayer. All around him people, who were also wandering through, looked in surprise and whispered to each other. Most of the comments were friendly, although many were ignorant of what he was doing. But Rabbi Hertzberg felt the old cold feeling creeping over him. One or two comments reminded him only too strongly why he was here. When his prayers were over he stumbled out of the old castle tower meaning to set off down the winding streets of York to his hotel.

As the rabbi left the Tower, he was overcome by grief. He felt his legs give way beneath him and he began to fall. He was caught by a young black man, Tom Matthews, who led him to one side to recover. 'What happened?' Tom asked, frightened by the rabbi's pale and grief-lined face. 'Why have you been praying in the Tower. I saw you there. What is it all about?'

'I will tell you, but you may not understand. On 11 March 1185, urged on by some priests, a mob rushed through York killing any Jews they found.'

'What here, in York? But why?' said Tom, astonished by what the rabbi said.

'A mixture of fear of the outsider, greed (because one of the few jobs Jews were allowed to do was lending money) and religious hatred. Let me continue. As the turmoil and murder grew, a group of Jewish families took refuge in that old tower, Clifford's Tower. They had hoped they would be safe there, but they were discovered and the mob tried to storm the walls of the Tower. For a while the Jews defended themselves, hoping help would come from some of their friends in York. But no help came. On the morning of the seventh day, their rabbi, Rabbi Yom Tov Levy, stood before them all. He knew the situation was desperate. So he told them that just as God gave us life, so let us return that life to God.'

'What did he mean?' asked Tom.

'He was telling them that they should kill themselves,' replied Rabbi Hertzberg.

'But that's terrible!' said Tom.

'They were as good as dead anyway. Once the mob got to them, they would be brutally murdered. Better to be killed swiftly by those who love you,' replied the rabbi.

'During the night Rabbi Yom Tov Levy spoke to all those in the Tower. And one by one they came forward, having said goodbye to each other, and the rabbi cut their throats. A small group refused to come forward because they were afraid to die and said they would convert to Christianity to save their lives. When all those who were willing to die for their faith had been killed by the rabbi, he was left to kill himself. Can you even begin to imagine the depth of pain and sadness that great man must have felt? Then he plunged the dagger into his own throat. Later that day the mob broke in and even they were shocked by what they saw; and the Jews who thought that they would be safe if they converted to Christianity were massacred by the mob as they left the tower.'

'But why did you come here then if it is so distressing?' asked Tom.

'Because they suffered and I feel their suffering. I pray for their souls and I think of all those who have died at the hands of others over the centuries. I think of the attacks even today on our synagogues, on our cemeteries and upon our people. Do you understand?' the rabbi suddenly asked Tom, an anxious look in his eyes.

'More than you may know,' replied Tom. 'I have also suffered from racism and from hatred and violence. I know what you mean. But let me ask you a question. What have your people learned from the past and from this racism and intolerance?'

The rabbi looked up sharply. 'You ask a hard question, my friend. What have we learned indeed? Pray God, we should have learned what prejudice does to people. Many of us have. But not all. I look at Israel today and I want to weep. Most people in Israel want to live in peace with their fellow countryfolk, with the Palestinians. But not all. There are forces at work in Israel which remind me of the mob in York, the Crusaders in Mainz, the Cossacks in Poland in the seventeenth century or the Nazis in the Second World War. There is something about power which corrupts even the best at times. Put them in a situation of power and fear and you have the most terrible combination. But we must never forget the good people, those who hid Jews here in York, in Speier, in Poland and in Germany. I suppose what my people have learned most of all is that only the fool dismisses an entire people.'

Information boxes

Cossacks in Seventeenth-Century Poland

In 1644 two Russian groups, the Cossacks and the Tartars, rose against the Jews living in Russia and also against the Roman Catholics of Poland. The Russian troops were gradually joined by bands of Russian peasants. Throughout the year Jewish and Polish towns were ransacked and invaded. A small proportion of the Jews were taken captive but many thousands of Jews and Poles were tortured and murdered. The only Jews and Poles to escape were those who renounced their religion and entered the Christian Orthodox faith. The violent persecutions continued for 18 months until a peace treaty was declared. After that many, who had become Orthodox Christians rather than be killed, were allowed to return to their own faith. However, this peace was temporary and war broke out again in 1651.

Chagall painted many scenes of the persecution of Jews in Eastern Europe

The Massacre at Mainz

As the peasant armies of the First Crusade set out for the Holy Land in 1096, some of them decided to destroy the Jewish communities they met on the way.

One of the worst massacres was at the German city of Mainz. The Archbishop ordered the city gates to be shut to protect the Jews against the wild mob of peasant crusaders. However, anti-Jewish riots broke out in the city. The rioters opened the city gates to the Crusaders. The Jews took refuge in the Archbishop's palace, but when the mob attacked this, the Archbishop fled and most of the Jews were massacred. It is said over a thousand Jews were murdered at Mainz in two days.

The Council for Racial Equality

The Council for Racial Equality was set up by the Race Relations Act of 1976 with the aims of:

- working to urge the elimination of discrimination
- promoting equality of opportunity and good relations between persons of different racial groups generally
- keeping under review the working of the Act and when required by the Secretary of State, or when it otherwise thinks necessary, to draw up and submit to the Secretary of State proposals for amending it.

The address of the Council for Racial Equality is Elliot House, 10–12 Allington Street, London SW1 E5EH.

Activities

1. Why did the visiting rabbi feel ill in the tower?
2. What experiences do you think Tom and the young rabbi had in common?
3. At certain Jewish festivals songs of sadness called laments are sung. Write a lament about the deaths in the tower.

The 800th anniversary of the events at Clifford's Tower

Sources

BUDDHISM

The Buddha taught 'Let not one deceive another nor despise any person whatsoever. In anger and ill-will let not one wish any harm to another.' Through meditation Buddhists begin to see how they unconsciously try to cover up their own fears, insecurities and self-dislike by projecting it all onto other people. Acting as a group, chanting slogans and abuse at others, can give people a feeling of strength and security, regardless of any personal troubles or beliefs. Whatever rights and wrongs there may be, this kind of behaviour only obscures them and makes it difficult to find solutions.

Buddhists meditate on kindness and loving concern for others and even their enemies. Buddhists acknowledge and reflect on their feelings of dislike or even hatred. They then try to change them to feelings of kindness, understanding and compassion. It must be acknowledged that Buddhists are not always successful in this, and there are examples of racial persecution in Buddhist countries.

But Tibet, a Buddhist country, is threatened with destruction by its Chinese conquerors. Its leader-in-exile, the Dalai Lama, has stood firm on the view not to answer violence and racism with more violence and racism. This would destroy the very Buddhist values which the Tibetan people are striving to defend and uphold. The Tibetan resistance has been almost entirely non-violent, and the spirit of the people remains unbroken even after many years of terrible oppression. For Buddhism teaches that 'never by hatred is hatred dissolved . . . One should conquer anger through kindness, wickedness through goodness, selfishness through charity, and lying through speaking the truth.'

CHRISTIANITY

The Roman Catholic Church teaches that racism is a sin. There is no question on this, and along with the Roman Catholic Church, most Protestant Churches agree with this. Indeed, through the World Council of Churches Programme to Combat Racism, the churches have given money to thousands of groups, mostly non-Christian ones, who have fought or are fighting against racism.

In South Africa, while the official church, the Dutch Reformed Church, did support apartheid for a period, it was the other churches which led the fight against that form of racism.

The foundation for the Christian belief that all people are equal before God and one another comes from the Bible. In Galatians 3:28, St Paul puts it very clearly. In Christ 'There is neither Jew nor Greek, slave nor freeman, neither male nor female: for you are all one in Christ Jesus.'

The Christian faith accepts all people as equal and anything which is raised as a barrier against this is a sin against the unity that God has given us. In recent centuries, racism has crept into the Western churches through imperialism and other forces. To try and deal with this, the churches have recently made their teachings plainly known, such as the Roman Catholics in their document on Racism produced by the Justice and Peace Secretariat, and have in many places funded anti-racist campaigns within the churches to help overcome racism.

JUDAISM

Jews have suffered terribly from racism over the centuries, and lost one third of their people in the space of six years this century under Nazi rule in Germany and Eastern Europe. Jews are therefore totally against racism and have been predominant in anti-racist movements throughout the world, including South Africa and in the civil rights movement in the USA.

In Jewish teaching marriage with someone of another faith is wrong, but that is because of religious differences and would apply whatever the colour of the skin of the spouse. Once conversion to Judaism has taken place there is no bar to marriage on grounds of race.

One of the greatest passages in the whole of the Bible is the account in the Book of Genesis, chapter 10, of the families of the nations. The remarkable feature of this passage is the description of all the known peoples of the world as descended from the three sons of Noah and therefore forming one huge family. The belief in God as the Creator of the world and the father of all men and women involves a belief in the brotherhood of human beings. Judaism is therefore completely against racism on the basis that we are all God's creatures, and it looks forward to a Messianic age when all people recognise their brotherhood under one God.

ISLAM

Racism, whether open or disguised, is an evil aspect of life which Islam seeks to eradicate. It is clear from verses in the Qur'an and some of the sayings of the Prophet Muhammad, that differences in colour, race or traditions are not to be used as excuses for unjust treatment:

> And among His signs is the creation of the heavens and the earth, and the variations in your language and your colours; verily, in that there are Signs for those who know.
> (Qur'an, chapter 30, verse 22)

The Hajj, the annual pilgrimage to Makkah, is a prime example of the multiracial aspect of Islam. Muslims of all colours, from all over the world, gather with one common purpose, to worship Allah. Muslims are not a distinct racial or ethnic group to be classified as 'Asians' or 'Arabs' to the exclusion of the others.

Role-play

1. Imagine that the United Nations has called a World Enquiry on racism. The United Nations (UN) is alarmed at the pain, suffering and distress caused in so many parts of the world by racism. You have to come to the Enquiry to present your case as to why racism is wrong. Looking at the stories or at the sources, choose either a person from one of the stories, such as the Tibetan monk, or a faith, such as Christianity. If you choose a character, tell the story in your own words but most important of all, make one point from the story which you think everyone needs to understand in order to stop racism. If you choose a faith, tell the key points of that faith's attitude to racism, but also highlight just one of these teachings which you think should be heard by everyone in order to stop racism. Now prepare a case to put before the Enquiry. It must be short – no more than two minutes.

   The whole class then becomes the Enquiry. As each person reports their story, a scribe needs to take down the main point which the Enquiry feels comes out of the story or account given. At the end, make recommendations to be adopted by world governments. These recommendations should be based upon the

United Nations General Assembly Hall

one point each person raised in their accounts. Such a statement should be short with a clear set of points. Once you have finished it, send it to the British Ambassador to the UN in New York and ask for his/her response.

2. In some countries, governments have decided that to help minority groups such as members of minority religions, or people from a minority racial background, they must have positive discrimination. This means that the laws set out to make it easier for such people to get jobs, go to college and so on. This is done to help them defeat the old patterns of behaviour by which a majority group will tend to look after its own members, for example, with better housing, health, jobs, education opportunities, etc. So, in some cases, governments have said that a certain percentage of places in college must be filled by minority group members. For example, if there were 15 per cent of the people in a country from a different religion, then the government might insist that 15 per cent of places in universities and colleges should be filled by members of that religion. This may mean that students from a minority group may get in with grades which are lower than college standards. It can also mean that some members of the majority group with better grades do not get a place.

First of all, what do you think of this idea? Is it fair or right to do this? Do you think it will help race relations?

Secondly, in groups, take the position on racism given by one of the faiths and work out what you think they might say about positive discrimination. Try to follow what you understand the teachings to be saying.

Index